LIVING
on the
PLAIN

LIVING
on the
PLAIN
THE GOSPEL OF LUKE

Mike Stone

CHURCH
PUBLISHING
INCORPORATED

Unless otherwise noted, the scripture quotations are from New Revised Standard Version Bible, copyright © 1989 National Council of the Churches of Christ in the United States of America. Used by permission. All rights reserved worldwide.

Church Publishing
19 East 4th Street
New York, NY 10016
www.churchpublishing.org

Cover design by Jennifer Kopec, 2Pug Design
Typeset by PerfecType, Nashville, Tennessee

A record of this book is available from the Library of Congress.
ISBN: 978-1-64065-330-6 (paperback)
ISBN: 978-1-64065-331-3 (ebook)

CONTENTS

ACKNOWLEDGMENTS

Huge thanks to Church Publishing and for the kind and thorough guidance of my editors, Sharon Pearson and Wendy Barrie. The Rev. David Peters made this book possible, encouraging me from a relatively cold call on publishing in general and throughout the publication process, as both tutor and comforter. Lila Anderson, Tim Brown, and Hal Snapp helped me to have the heart to try and make private writings public.

The congregation of St. Thomas the Apostle in Nassau Bay, Texas, was the guinea pig and tester of much of my work and they, like the wonderful people of Christ Church in Coronado, California, and St. Alban's in El Cajon, California, mentored me not only in faithful ministry, but in faithful humanity and nourished both my call and creativity. The Very Rev. Edward Harrison fathered my voice as a priest and called forth from me my own story, without which this book would not have been possible. My clergy colleagues in both Texas and San Diego have called for the best in me and the vision of Bishop Andy Doyle for Brené Brown's Daring Way literally changed the quality and quantity of my life.

My teachers at Gardner-Webb University and Candler School of Theology provided not only content, but a structure and support for content to sink in, become transformative, and seep back out into the world. I am especially grateful for the humility and care of Steve Kraftchick and Neil Walls, the encouragement of Ted Hackett to chance my vocational plans for the better, the extreme patience and accompaniment of Kent Blevins, the intentional inclusion of Gerald Keown, and the maturity modeled by Tom Jones.

Lastly, my family, both parents who spoke their truth in love, children, Daniel and Emory, who revealed the awe and wonder of God's universe, and my partner and spouse, Rebecca, who still makes me want to be a better person eighteen years later and continues to serve as holy mirror, mentor, and foundation. Thanks for teaching me to speak and believing that my voice might be life-giving to someone else.

Introduction

Taste and See

I was fifteen years old before I was willing to try salsa. It wasn't exactly by choice; I was preoccupied with weight as a high school wrestler and Pace Picante Sauce had almost no effect on my mass, was high in fiber, and was close enough to pasta sauce that it made baked tortilla chips semiedible. Within a few years, I discovered guacamole, although it took a major friend's urging to get me to try some. Then it was sour cream. (I had given up wrestling by then!) Finally, it was refried beans. They all came together for me in my midtwenties at a Costco food sampling: six-layer dip (the cheese was always there for me). I am so grateful now that I was pushed out of my comfort zone with salsa, let alone the guac, but to weave together six different dips in one—what a symphony of flavor! Then I met seven-layer dip. Olives on top. A little fruity. Another flavor to learn and to synthesize.

I was raised in the church with flannel boards, memory verses, youth group, Vacation Bible School, service projects, and thrice-weekly services. I savored the Bible daily. As a college freshman, I realized within two weeks of my Introduction to the Old Testament class that I had only acquired one flavor of reading and understanding the Bible when there were many others in the world, flavors that could stimulate not only my mental palate, but my spirit, my body, my relationships. New flavors gave my spirituality new kinds of nutrition and energy. New flavors expanded my world.

The Gospel of Luke has its own distinct flavors: inclusion of women, concern for the poor and outcast, and plain living among all of God's family. To that, add the general flavors of academic Bible study: layers like etymology, source criticism, archaeology, and psychological criticism, to name a few. Together, these flavors make the call to discipleship even more robust, taking on new depths, applications, and challenges. It is my hope that some of these flavors will be new, stimulating, and nourishing. If one gives you heartburn, move on. If it nourishes your spirit, eat up and follow a Jesus who is always bigger than we've settled for!

Living on the Plain is divided into fifty-eight separate reflections on portions from the Gospel of Luke. Not every detail is covered; nor is every story. To make the most of this journey, begin with the citation at the top of each chapter. Read Luke's story and consider what it means for you. Where are you in the story? What do you wish Luke had added or subtracted? What might Luke be calling you toward for your own sake and for the sake of the world? Avoid the study notes in your Bible! Read the text first and someone else's thoughts, including mine, second. You can read *Living on the Plain* as a two-month personal, daily meditation, or divided into chunks as you see fit—some reflections might need more than a day to engage. Each reflection has several embedded questions. The reader might want to answer these in a journal, in the margins, or throw them out all together and ask their own. Groups might enjoy *Living on the Plain* by sharing responses to the embedded questions, while preachers might consider these questions as Luke's opportunities for the contemporary disciple. Taste at your own pace and I pray that *Living on the Plain* enhances your faith palette!

God-Lovers

Read Luke 1:1–4

Luke's beginning targets both his audience and purpose, and thereby offers a target for our own journey, both through the book and into faith. Tradition identifies Luke as the physician who shared time with Paul on a missionary journey, as described in the Acts of the Apostles, the second of Luke's writings. If so, Luke was not an eyewitness to the events he describes and has collected sayings and stories of Jesus, likely using Mark's Gospel as an outline and another yet-to-be-discovered document that the evangelist Matthew also seemed to have used (commonly known as "Q").

Luke organized each story or saying as a brushstroke in his portrait of who Jesus is and what he means. There is an Eastern tradition that locates Luke as the first iconographer and that Luke's representations of the saints and Jesus himself are not only traditional, but historically accurate. Understanding Luke as an iconographer is a helpful approach as we begin our study, as icons are not prayed to, but prayed through. Their gaze is meant to help the viewer search themselves and search out the grace of God through the saint depicted: in this case, Jesus. In writing his account for Theophilus, Luke acknowledges the stories about Jesus have already been presented by many.

Theophilus may have been a friend or acquaintance of Luke, but was more likely a general address. "Theophilus" is a Greek compound that is best translated "God-lover." Luke writes an account of Jesus's life and ministry and what it might mean for the future of humanity to these God-lovers. In reading this book, consider yourself in part of Luke's audience. Not sure if you love God enough? No worries. God-lover may mean something like "curious enough to do some sniffing-out after." As a college student, I heard about the ministry of a particular Ivy League chaplain who was frequently confronted by brazen students confronting his piety with the challenge, "I don't believe in God." The wise chaplain, so the story goes, took a deep breath and asked with palpable curiosity and patient follow-through, "Tell me what kind of God you don't believe in; I probably don't believe in that one either." Perhaps God-lover doesn't mean contemporary Christian consumer, cloistered monastic, or denominationally branded, confessed, confirmed, and communicated Christian. Perhaps it describes folks who wonder about life, love, justice, and peace, and what they have to do with humanity and things greater than ourselves. In this sense, Luke does not write to a single person, to pious people, or a church, but to all. Luke writes to give his account of Jesus to people who wonder, precisely because there were so many other versions of the story that Luke believed did not meet the needs of God-lovers or of God.

What will *our* Lukan journey be about? Could it be bearing witness in a culture saturated with often competing and incoherent stories about who Jesus was and who he would become and how he would act in today's world? It's almost as if Luke is inviting us to pen our own gospel to the world through how we live our lives. There are competing and incoherent stories about the Lord in the many Gospel accounts, both authorized and those accounts found outside the New Testament canon. How will be we bear witness to the truth?

Does God delight in compassion or judgment? What do we delight in? Does God help those who help themselves? Do we help the helpless? Does God forgive begrudgingly or with fanfare and celebration? Does God hate the same people we do? Luke invites us to live the answers to these questions more deeply than we ever have before for the "God-lover" inside each of us. Luke offers another opportunity to live into our theology of grace so that our family, friends, and neighbors can experience the truth about Jesus that they already know all too well in story, but may have yet to experience in life. Luke frames a chance to air our own curiosities, hopes, doubts, and confusions about what the gospel means for the twenty-first century: its challenges, doubt, and losses. God-lover, God-doubter, God-curious, God-disappointed, let us "Luke" at Jesus together and live on the plain of faith more deeply.

2

Unexpected Messengers

Read Luke 1:5–25

This reading offers many seemingly unrelated insights that comically (in the Shakespearean sense) weave together. Perhaps Luke is offering us insights into the tapestries of our own lives.

Zechariah and Elizabeth are blameless and righteous, but barren. They do not deserve to have their hopes disappointed, nor to be disgraced by their community, as Elizabeth summarizes. Rather, these should be ideal folk, looked up to not only for their lineage, but their fidelity and piety. A cultural expectation gets in the way of people appreciating who they are. Perhaps it gets in the way of their appreciating themselves. They could just as well have a child with mental illness or one who grows up and ends up incarcerated or loses their job with no severance, and so on. It is often easy to conclude that something is inherently wrong with people who do not meet cultural norms. Zechariah and Elizabeth defy our "get-what-you-pay-for" stereotyping. As we begin our reexamination of Luke, Jesus, and faith, can we wonder how people carry their burdens instead of condemning the burdens they carry?

Zechariah is a priest who has trouble hearing and believing God. There is hope for us! Priests, then as now, are no better or more pious than anyone else, but simply feel called to perform a particular role in community life and enough people recognize and consent to their call.

Angels might be costumed or in disguise today. Angel means "messenger" in Greek—like a singing telegram, a network newscaster, or a barista at Starbucks. This messenger happens to be Gabriel, who stands in God's presence, but Zechariah does not seem to know that. Did angels have wings or halos? In art they do, so we can visually distinguish them from the saints and other characters. In the Hebrew Bible, superhuman beings seems to come in three types: giants; the seraphim, winged serpents perpetually ablaze; and cherubim, four-faced (lion, ox, eagle, human), eyeball-covered beings with three sets of wings. (Maybe that's why they always start their messages with "Do not be afraid.") What if angel messengers looked just like us? What if they actually *were* us? Maybe Zechariah sees Gabriel as a mortal because Gabriel is one, an arch-messenger, one who offers God's thoughts to others. After all, aren't the prophets also just messengers? Wasn't Martin Luther King Jr. a messenger from God in so many ways? This is not to say that there are not supernatural beings in God's household, but that maybe angels are simply messengers from God. What message would God have us deliver on a spiritual journey to the barren and ridiculed? Could we be angels? Would we be believable?

Zechariah is wordless after hearing the news he had always yearned for but had increasingly lost hope in. Maybe he was being chastened or maybe he was just speechless at grace. When was the last time you were speechless at grace, filled with awe and wonder, knocked down by the love of another not because you felt unworthy, but because the weight of their love took your breath away? "I don't know what to say" is, after all, a message. One of my best friends insists that it takes at least ten seconds of silence to absorb a compliment. Could we discipline ourselves to be speechless when presented with grace in any form?

Will the son Zechariah and Elizabeth always wanted also be the one they hoped for? Children are not commodities. Their son, John, does not grow up to be a venerated priest, but a guy standing on a city corner wearing a sandwich board that reads, "The end is near." He grows up to be intentionally homeless and wears a hair shirt inside out. He eats weird food. He challenges political leaders and loses his head. The narrative is blank, but I sure hope that Zechariah and Elizabeth were proud of their boy. Can we make room for God's surprises to come in packages that confront our norms and the scripts we have imagined for even years on end?

Maybe all of these threads are just trying to make the supernatural more accessible, offering us opportunities to be speechless at everyday grace, to wonder when confronted by disappointment, to make room for empathy, and to grow into appreciation for one another. I hope so.

3

Grace without Strings

Read Luke 1:26–38

As a child I always wondered why it took God so long to come up with the idea of Jesus. More specifically, I had been duly instructed that without Jesus to take away our sins, we were going to hell. What did that mean for all the people who were born, sinned, and died before the coming of Jesus? What about the prophets, patriarchs, and matriarchs? Was their best only good enough to get them on the flannel board of the Sunday school room and not into God's rest?

Compassionate Sunday school teachers and pastors got me off the hook here: those people's sins somehow got pushed forward onto Jesus, who took care of the past and the present. But did they live believing they had to work their way into God's favor, missing out on an understanding of God's grace? Some believe we all have ended up in this same plight; unless we do the work of accepting Jesus, we don't get to have the grace that comes with belief. I remember learning that God is especially mad at people who hear about Jesus and reject grace by not accepting him as their personal Lord and Savior through the sinner's prayer. God gives a gift and we have to accept it. It's not work, I was taught; it is like taking the keys to a new Ferrari (hardly work to reach out and receive something so valuable without paying for it), only hell is on the line if you don't accept it.

I give gifts like that. I have nuggets of wisdom, strategy, and training programs to burn fat and build muscle, whether literal or figurative, that sure would make people's lives better. If they don't want to take what I am giving, then they don't deserve them. I help people I don't know sometimes, with money or gift cards, but I make them know that it is important how they use my gifts of grace, because if they don't really need charity, they have no business receiving it.

Surely God does not give as we do. Surely gifts are given to be enjoyed or neglected, invested in or left fallow, displayed or enjoyed, not because of what we will or will not do with them, but out of the intention behind them. Strings are attached to investments, rentals, leases, and loans. Gifts really are the property of the recipient, even if unopened or underappreciated. I am trying to grow into being a giver instead of an investor or landlord, and Luke can help me.

In Luke's story, Mary gets quite an opportunity: join the unwed teenage mothers' club. This is not a story about God's gracious gifts, but about God's call to a ministry of grace. God's grace was assured for Mary no matter what she said. God's grace in the person of Jesus came through Mary precisely because she chose to work with God, even at her own expense, to suffer a scandal she didn't earn or deserve on behalf of the very people who would likely deride, ridicule, and mock her. Maybe the reason so much time passed between the expulsion from Eden and birth of the Lord is that all the other women God approached had said no. Maybe Mary was just the first one to say, "Yes."

Maybe discipleship is more about saying "Yes" to God than "No" to sugar. "Maybe," as Jack Johnson sings, "pretty much always means no." Martin Luther had his own phrase: "How often 'not now' becomes never." If God's grace is assured, might we be willing to say "Yes" to God's latest seemingly cockamamie scheme for revealing grace and life for the world? Maybe our "yes," our participation with God in grace distribution, isn't really about whether or not we are given grace, but whether or not we choose to open the gift and enjoy it. If a messenger from God, whether Gabriel, your crazy Uncle Steve, or your annoying coworker stands before you and asks if you will join God's conspiracy to help the world be open to the grace God freely offers, could your Lukan discipline be to answer, "Yes"?

The Model Mary

Read Luke 1:39–45

John the Baptist and his mother, Elizabeth, model empathy. As a child, I learned that empathy and sympathy are synonyms, but having experienced and offered each, I am confident that they are worlds apart.

Elizabeth (and John, still in the womb) rejoice with Mary. For a teenage girl, unmarried, pregnant, and possibly "visiting" her cousin in order to escape stoning in her home village, safety must have been paramount. Elizabeth and Zechariah not only offer sanctuary in their home, but the opportunity to experience the potential that there may be more than grief and panic; there may also be feelings of hopefulness, blessedness, and connection with her body. They do not try and talk Mary out of her feelings, but within a safe space, offer to help realize feelings that she was not even aware of. We are not always in positions of offering physical sanctuary, but we are confronted with uncountable daily opportunities to offer empathy as sanctuary instead of the sympathy we so often settle for.

Sym-pathy: Feeling like someone else. Usually ends up being competitive. Can lead to "conversational narcissism" where we try to connect with someone else's experience by offering our own as proof that we have real street cred in the school of hard knocks. When someone is hurting, sympathy talks over them so that they know they are not alone. Sympathy often tries to talk people out of the intensity of their feeling by comparing

9

it to our own. "I know your parents are driving you crazy, but at least you still have your parents; mine died when I was ten." *At least* often appears in the sympathy script and is usually the harbinger of a backhanded sign of support, like beginning a sentence with "I love her to death, but . . ." Sympathy follows this bull into the china shops of grief and loss and actually ends up begging for the one in need of care to offer it. Sympathy sees someone at the bottom of a dark hole—afraid, possibly hurt, and unable to see well—and discusses other holes. Sympathy is about feeling like someone else, which is pretty hard to do, even for identical twins, because, well, there are just so many variables in our experience. We can never prove that our surviving cancer presages everyone else doing so, that our moving past the death of our spouse of fifty-three years means everyone will have the same outcome.

Em-pathy. Feeling with. Connects with human base more than the exact details. All of us are equipped to empathize because we have all experienced loss, pain, betrayal, celebration. Getting in tune with our experience allows us to imagine and connect with someone else's, even if the particulars vary wildly. Empathy seeks to understand, not to compare. Empathy seeks to make room for the story and experience of another above all else. Empathy says, often without words, that I am here with you, able to make space for your grief and loss and joy—for you—in my own, different life. Empathy validates the feelings that we have that we are rarely in control of. Empathy asks: Tell me more. Starts with, "I have no idea how you might be feeling." Middles at, "I want to be with you right now." And ends when the other person tells us they are done, not when we are done. Empathy is when we see another at the bottom of a hole, tie a rope around our waist so that we do not fall irretrievably into the same hole (where's the help in that?), and join them.

Elizabeth's end line seems the crux of faith—to trust that God will fulfill our lives. The hardest thing for me in relationships is knowing whether or not my love or effort is going to "work." Will it make a difference? I could withstand tutoring bills, daily commutes, endless picking-up-after, homework, medicine reminders, or on and on if I knew that we were going to get where I knew we needed to go. Maybe Elizabeth is offering us an image as we begin this journey through Luke; we are invited to trust that in the end, God *is* going to catch and hold us no matter how unsteady we feel or are. What if we could live our lives backward, certain that God will catch us? If only we could be certain that our efforts regarding our spouses, children, parents, coworkers, and others *are* going to carry these folks into larger life, that God is able to accomplish more than we can ask or imagine. Maybe the fall into grace could be something that we enjoy instead of something that makes us hyperventilate. Maybe that fall could open us to empathy and grace, knowing that God's outcome is assured. Maybe peeking ahead spoils the ending. But maybe the ending enriches the way we live our own story.

5

A Real Birth Story

Luke 2:1–7

Here is the story of Christ's birth that we see in children's Christmas pageants. However, there are a few hidden details of the all-too-familiar Christmas story that tend to be overlooked.

In the Roman census, men were to be counted, not women. Why does Mary accompany Joseph? It could be that Joseph wanted to be present for the delivery of the child, but perhaps even more critical he wanted to make sure Mary was *not* in Nazareth when the child was born due to the threat of honor killings for women pregnant out of wedlock. Mary chooses the danger of a week's journey on donkey's back to staying put. Are there ways we put women or others—with our stereotypes, jokes, or policies—in double-bind positions that force such difficult choices?

The New Revised Standard Version of the Bible uses the word "engaged." The King James is a little more accurate with "betrothed." Betrothal happened in the ancient world when a man compensated the bride's father for having raised her; the bride-price was remunerating the dad for having fed and clothed a girl who could neither carry on the family name nor inherit property. Women did not pay dowries at the time of Jesus; men paid the bride price. Joseph paid for Mary at their betrothal, but possession did not happen until the wedding. A pregnancy during betrothal could have been a sign of infidelity or an unchastity of the worst kind, as illegitimacy inhibited a child's inheritance rights. Joseph has spent his life savings on Mary (notice Joseph is a fairly passive figure in Luke, as compared to Matthew), only to have his firstborn son a compromised inheritor. Do we similarly put restrictions around the inheritance of grace that God wills for each of us? When I was a child, divorced persons were not allowed to serve on the board of the church. Some denominations don't allow the divorced to receive communion. The point here is not what these folks do, but about what we do with this in mind.

Men were not typically present for childbirth in the ancient world, any more than they were in the 1950s. Menstruation and childbirth rendered a woman ritually unclean, and that uncleanliness was viewed as contagious, so it is unlikely Joseph attended the birth. Do we let cultural understandings of uncleanliness get in the way of connection?

Joseph's family was from Bethlehem and it would have been a tremendous insult for him to stay at an inn instead of a relative's home, even if there was room. Archaeology suggests that families in Bethlehem lived in cave grottos instead of a "proper" village, but Luke is telling a "village" story. My family functions similarly—we slept on the couches at our grandparents if there were no beds, or atop blankets on the floor. When you visited family, they housed and fed you. "Inn" is a translation possibility, but so is "room." It seems likely that the holy family visited a relative and, because of the census calling all men to be counted, the home was already occupied, so they stayed in an area of the home where the animals were kept. Barns were not erected in cities (if at all). Mangers were indeed stone food troughs and likely positioned so that animals could eat without bending their heads to the ground. Hay is what mattresses were made of anyway, so putting a baby there (my daughter slept most comfortably in a box when she was born because of convenience and size) was pretty reasonable.

Maybe Jesus was born lowlier than most, laid in a food trough in a barn. There is truth to God descending to earth in lowliness instead of luxury. Luke might be suggesting that Jesus was incarnated in the most ordinary of ways: a home birth in a time when there were no hospitals, animals, and relatives all around and swaddled for his comfort, as was standard practice. Home births were not normal when I was born, hospital births were. It is almost as though Luke is saying that God took on flesh in Good Samaritan Hospital in Lexington, Kentucky, and was laid in a nursery bed next to the infant Michael Stone. What a miracle to find God in the ordinary! What a challenge from Luke for our lives; Jesus could be fully vested in the people in our midst—someone in line at Starbucks, doing yoga next to us, or even those who drive too fast and pass us on the right. Greg Boyle, founder of Homeboy Industries, shares: "Jesus doesn't lose any sleep that we will forget that the Eucharist is sacred. He is anxious that we might forget it is ordinary, that it is a meal shared among friends. And that's the incarnation."[1] Perhaps Luke is asking us to consider that those moments when our neighbor seems utterly devoid of the holy are not their moments of abject failure, but precisely when our imagination has failed us and instead we might look for Jesus to be right in a messy hay pile surrounded by ungroomed animals.

---

1. Greg Boyle, interview with Krista Tippett, *On Being*, NPR, February 13, 2013, https://onbeing.org/programs/greg-boyle-the-calling-of-delight-gangs-service-and-kinship/.

6

Holy Recognition

Luke 2:21–38

The Book of Common Prayer includes the Song of Simeon twice in the Daily Office—as a canticle option during Morning Prayer and just before the concluding versicle for Compline. Certainly, the prayer book is inviting us at Morning Prayer to see God's salvific, life-giving actions in the scripture readings. Even more, the prayer book invites us at the close of each day to rest in peace, assured that we have seen God's salvation in the course of the day, no matter how bad, disappointing, mundane, or celebratory it was.

Simeon's song was not a once-upon-a-time declaration, but an invitation to examine our day and our life with the assurance that God was, is, and will be present, working on what is best for us; if we cannot see God's saving work in our day, it is our vision that is lacking and not God's presence. Seeing might be believing, but the prayer book and Luke, as we shall see in chapter 16, suggest that believing is seeing, that our trust determines what becomes apparent for us. If we think that life is tough and then you die, it is likely that we will see that bleakness played out. If, on the other hand, if we trust that the universe conspires toward the meeting of our personal destiny, as Paulo Coelho suggests in *The Alchemist*, we might see God working all things, even our challenges, to the good of those who love God (Rom. 8:28).

More specifically, Simeon invites us to consider that God's saving work could be embodied in someone we meet today and that God's work, once again, includes the care, concern, and hope for "Gentiles": people different from us, "nonbelievers," people with dubious hygiene, people with different customs and holidays, people who eat strange foods and may not watch football or like barbeque.

Simeon is an old man, a man on the edge of dying. A stranger to Mary, he picks up her baby. Anna (notice that Luke continues to include women) is an old, even ancient, woman who is essentially homeless, living in a modern-day cathedral—the Temple. These two individuals recognize Jesus for who he is and what he means, even though they, once again, challenge our biases against strangers, the elderly, and the homeless. Hmm. Maybe they behave the way we think these folks might—babbling about the hope of a baby, something we might dismiss as crazy talk or senility. But this time, they are right. And Luke insists they be in the story. Perhaps they just are without guile, which always sounds crazy when you are expecting tact and manners instead of revelation and truth. I survive compliments I consider effusive pretty well by dismissing them this way . . . but what if I let them in? What if we all did?

If you are looking to find a spiritual practice in Luke, praying the Song of Simeon at the end of the day and then remembering the activities and insights, the conversations and happenings of the day, with an eye toward salvation moments, may be a holy one. Called by Ignatians the Examen, this is a gratitude practice that can help retrain our minds and spirits to remember events according to their light and God's palpable presence, instead of according to our disappointments, unmet appetites, and jealousies. It is holy work. It is work. It means replacing the sheep counting or imagining how you might spend lottery earnings or whatever it is that helps you fall to sleep with a different funnel for your mind—but one that also guides your spirit.

7

In God's House

Luke 2:39–52

Luke is the only Gospel with a story of the boy Jesus that actually made it into the Bible. Interestingly, there are a number of Jesus-as-a-boy stories, some of them quite old, that belong mostly to a collection of works called the New Testament Pseudepigrapha (pseudo as in "false," epigraph as in "writing"). Copious ancient works were written and falsely attributed to celebrities and faith heroes. In the ancient imagination, it seems, the child Jesus was more than a bit petulant. In one such story, he was playing hide-and-seek with his friends. Jesus went looking for them and heard some noise. Entering the house, he asked the mom what the noises were. Not wanting to give the game away, she told the boy Jesus that these were just the goats. He responds by saying, "As you have spoken, so shall it be," claps his hands, and turned the children into goats. Word to the wise, play carefully with this one! Another lengthy cycle describes Jesus afflicting his various tutors with all kinds of ailments because they presumed to teach him something. Thank God these stories did not make it into scripture.

Luke's version could invite us into a flat read like those fairy tale stories of the God-boy Jesus. He could be telling his parents that since he is the child of God, he does not need to obey them when traveling and they should know this and be respectful. While this is the way I was taught to read the text, it doesn't even hold up in the story itself: Joseph and Mary are perplexed. As the story comes early in the Gospel, this might be an opportunity to reflect on a deep and sacred mystery: the two natures of Jesus. In Orthodox and Roman Christianity, the Council of Nicaea decided that Jesus was fully human and fully divine, paradoxical to be sure. Disagreeing Christian sects argued the Monophysite position, that Jesus only had the divine nature, but appeared to have the human (or vice versa.) Another splinter group, the Docetists, argued that God entered Jesus at baptism and left before the cross so that God did not have to suffer because they believed that God cannot suffer. Western Christianity, however, insists that Jesus was somehow fully human and divine; we have struggled to figure out how this could be true and expressed ever since. Human people do not walk into a room and read everyone else's minds. They don't do miracles. They get pimples on prom night, have indigestion and arthritis. God, on the other hand, probably never has a bad hair day, is all-knowing and all-powerful, and all-present. How on earth can these be possible?

In my own imagination, this can only work if the divine submits to the human. This is more than a Great Dane playing with a Chihuahua without demolishing it. Submission would mean holding back. It would mean that Jesus had to learn, did not automatically know where the kids were hiding during hide and seek, and that he might not have even really understood that Joseph was not his father. What if Jesus did not fully realize his own identity and had to figure it out in bits and pieces as he lived? He'd be more like me, or I'd be more like him for sure. What if Jesus, like Elijah, Elisha, and the disciples, doesn't perform miracles through his fingertips, but through his openness to God working through him? What if Jesus accepts every single human limitation and never overpowers a single one of them? Then he'd be exactly who the Epistle to the Hebrews 4:14–16 says he is: in perfect solidarity with humanity, in weakness and in strength.

Maybe Luke is sharing this story to tell us that Jesus took the term "father" seriously. As we will see in Luke's genealogy, even Adam is a child of God. Maybe this is not about challenging Joseph's authority, but Jesus exploring his greater family. Maybe Luke wants us to reconsider our relationship to God as well. Calling God a parent figure, Father or Mother, puts us in a special relationship. God not only cares for us as a creation, but as family members. Perhaps we truly dwell in our Father's house when we are aware not only of God's interest in us, but in God's curiosity and care. And maybe we dwell in our father's house when we treat other people as relatives in the family of God. In parallel paradox with the two natures of Jesus, maybe when we live fully into our humanity, we will find God more fully present than we ever thought possible. Pimples on prom night don't come only to the godless, but to children of God. Missing a free throw not only happens in the NBA, it happened to Jesus. Abusing the hell out of ourselves when we miss or trip or have a bad hair day seems the farthest thing from the incarnation Luke describes. Abusing the hell out of someone else for long fingernails or a moment of forgetfulness seems similarly far from dwelling in our Creator's house.

Take a moment to wonder about God's presence in the ordinary, in your day-to-day existence. Imagine God's family tree including your own, the neighbors, and the police officer who pulled you over. Take a moment to reimagine what the father's house is like: full of people. Full places get dirty real fast and lose the ability to screen applicants. Dwell there today, with them, with Jesus, with God.

8

Repent

Luke 3:1–6

L uke subtly changes the original quote from Isaiah 40:3 ("A voice of one calling, 'In the wilderness prepare the way for the LORD; make straight in the desert a highway for our God.' ") by having the voice call from the wilderness. Isaiah, written to the exiled Jewish community in Babylon, was likely talking about preparing the return route from Babylon to Jerusalem, a long journey with extremely varied "roads" that were more like trails at their best. Isaiah seems to know that God was going to accomplish a superhighway for those who were far from home so that they could return with safety and assurance. As with all super-highways, valleys would have to be exalted and high places strip-mined. God will bring those who have been removed from home quickly and efficiently back.

   Luke, however, puts John in the wilderness, in the deserted and dry places where life seems to hang in the balance. The desert is wild, its weather so unpredictable that drought can turn to flood in an instant. Food is fickle and scarce. John the Baptist lives on the margins of life, in the wilderness itself, and calls for a leveling, especially for those in the desert. If you know an alcoholic, you know someone who lives or has lived in the desert. If you know someone with an eating disorder, you know the des-ert. If you know a parent who has remorse about decisions they made for their kids years ago, someone who was downsized or furloughed without hope of finances coming predictably back online, someone who has lost a spouse, child, or friend, you know some of the deserts we find ourselves in. John goes to those places and proclaims that precisely there—specifically in the wildernesses of our lives—God is coming. And we should get ready so that we do not miss the joy of God's arrival: a baptism of repentance for the forgiveness of sins.

"Sin" comes to us from archery (*hattat* in Hebrew) and dramatic tragedy, the "tragic flaw" of a protagonist (*hamartia* in Greek). It can be roughly translated in both cases as "missing the mark." Sin implies that our aim was off, or perhaps we chose the wrong target. When we miss, we are certainly invited (and maybe expected) to shoot again, being careful to calibrate and discern our targets and adjust our aim. Do we sometimes settle for the good instead of the better? Do we aim for targets of our own comfort, or do we pause to consider where God might direct our efforts for the benefit of ourselves, others, for the world? The Book of Common Prayer (page 848) offers that sin is separation from God. Are there areas of our lives secluded from God? Can we even succeed in that endeavor if God is omnipresent, or do we rather live in untruth from time to time, buying into the false notion that God cannot and will not abide with us or the folks we dislike in our imperfections?

When we recalibrate our aim, we repent. "Repentance" comes from four alternate roots in Judeo-Christian tradition. The Hebrew word *shoov* is most literally translated as "turning" or "changing directions." We *shoov* when we turn our cars into the church parking lot, are interrupted by something greater than we had planned, give up an old practice, or adjust our goal setting. Shooving could be full of remorse, but could also be about living into our epiphanies or adopting holy habits. We shooved when we supported a capital funds drive (a turn from our ordinary stewardship), when we gave valentines to kids at a Title I school, and when we stop to enjoy our food instead of working through lunch.

The Greek word *metanoia*, from *meta* (beyond or above) and *nous* (worldview/law of thinking /schema), means to adopt a way of thinking that is beyond, above, greater than a previous way. It is not about learning truths as facts, but redrawing our perceptions around Truth. When personhood materializes out of prejudice, there is a new mind. When we drop our scrub brush that we had prepared to clean our neighbors and ourselves to make God less angry and instead break out the wine to celebrate God's presence in one another, there is a new mind. When we encounter the resurrected Jesus in the unclean, there is a new mind. When we love patiently, kindly, without envy or arrogance, there is a new mind.

The Latin word *poena*, the root of "penance," means making right what I did wrong, restoring the balance of honor and dignity that I upset. Apologies and contrition are important, but penance practices and shows a transformed life. A thief restores the principle with interest, like Zacchaeus. As Daniel Tiger (the newer, animated Mr. Rogers) sings: "Saying I'm sorry is the first step, then how can I help?"

The Hebrew word *niham* expresses deep grief in systemic sin. A parent grieves the poor choices of a child that they are powerless to stop because they know and love their child deeply and mourn the loss of larger life for them. When in my right mind, I am never embarrassed by my child—they make their own decisions, after all, as I make my own—but I certainly can be disappointed *for* them, for the elective pain they have taken up, often without knowing what they were incurring. God does this for humanity throughout the Bible. As a white, male, straight Episcopal priest, several studies suggest I will earn 12 percent more than a black man with my same credentials and have access to opportunities that my siblings of color will never be considered for. This is wrong, but how to fix it? Repenting of the benefit and privilege that is given me at the cost of others and being unable to change the system is *niham*. It is never completely corrective, but always compassionate.

The repentance that scripture, tradition, and reason call us toward, especially in Luke, is robust and four-fold. It levels low places and high and provides access to the Lord and to justice. John was washing people in a river to help them seek such fundamental change in vision and practice, changes that would prepare them for God's salvific presence in their various deserts.

Pray that part of your journey through Luke will be to welcome God into the rough places. John doesn't leave the desert, by the way. He does not become clothed in purple or rewarded with stock options or some other parting gift for his ministry. Anne Lamott offered, "God is not here to take away our suffering or our pain, but to fill it with his or her (God's) presence."[2] Make way for the Lord. If your spiritual discipline ever gets in the way, repent and give it up for Jesus!

2. Anne Lamott, *Traveling Mercies: Some Thoughts on Faith* (New York: Anchor Books, 1999), 241.

9

Abundance for All

Luke 3:7–17

John the Baptist elaborates on repentance as leveling and adjusting our aim. He begins by getting rid of the myth of special ancestry. Luke stresses our common ancestry, not our uncommon or individual one. The reason God can make children out of stones is that God made the stones along with the people.

The crowds are asked to share abundance with the needy. Parish thrift shops and partnerships with local schools, ministries to the chronically homeless and those locally "caught up short" live right into the imperative John is calling for: sharing extra clothes, backpacks, hygiene items, food, and more with people who have none. By sharing out of abundance, the low places of the world are made plain. It takes fill dirt from the mountains to bring this about; churches should continue to take aim at this target of God's and shoot straight. John asks us to repent of hoarding and aim for sharing.

Tax collectors were in a prime position to exploit people. Romans utilized Jewish persons to collect their revenues. As in all bureaucracies, if the central government wanted a dollar per person, the regional government would also need a dollar, as would the district and town and neighborhood levels. Add in the mandatory temple tax for the Judeans, which Rome helped collect (and stored debt records in the Jerusalem temple precincts), and the amount of taxation rose quickly. Tax collectors were empowered to collect the total due and anything else they could extract for themselves over and above. They were the Benedict Arnolds at the time of Jesus, commiserating with the enemy against their own people to soak in imperial favor while amassing wealth, using the threat of Roman soldiers/thugs when they came calling. John tells them to aim to collect the mandated minimum, not the personal maximum, and to suffer the disdain of their fellow countrymen and women without simultaneously profiting hand over fist. A tough ask in a world that could be feast or famine. Today's easy analogy would be the tax collector as the used car salesman—be honest and charge what is required, not whatever you can get. John is speaking to each of us as we collect what is owed, whether money, time, or honor, and to consider how we do it, when we do it, and if we shouldn't recalibrate our aim, whether it be gift exchanges, social parties, or whatever creative self-indictment John brings to you.

The soldiers' ability to extort monies is pretty clear and mafia-esque. John tells them to be satisfied with their wages as a means of repentance. Interesting and hard to hear. I doubt most of us resort to getting raises by means of threats or extortion. Satisfaction with wages? What about when we don't earn enough? What about when we could be earning more? This is a tough one to think through. A study a few years ago said wages have a positive linear relationship with happiness, until we earn $75,000.[3] After that point, the relationship is still positive, but no longer linear. Happiness plateaus and rises only very incrementally with pay. It is interesting to think that one of the ways we are most used to receiving and offering value in the workplace is through salary and that we therefore look, fairly naturally, for our salary as an estimation of our worth. Perhaps a Lukan discipline could be satisfaction with our wages. Or recalibrating our careers. Maybe a Lukan discipline could be satisfaction with the food in front of us instead of wishing for finer fare, better wine, and so on. The

3. Richard Carrier, "Money Buys Happiness? Not after You Hit Six Figures," *Richard Carrier Blogs*, April 7, 2018, https://www.richardcarrier.info/archives/13954.

difference between a good meal and a great meal is, more often than not, the mood I am in. Maybe we accept the wages and fare we have and avoid the inevitable blandness and disappointment that comes from imagining what we do not. How might this affect the way we treat ourselves, others, and the enjoyment of life?

John promises that one more powerful than he is coming, one who will immerse us not with water, but with fire and quench the chaff. Rather than accepting that some people are wholly wheat and others chaff, John is announcing that Jesus will be holier than John and us because he will be able to see the wheat in even the chaffiest person, loving that person into ridding the chaff. Isn't that the goal of salvation in the desert? To lose the heavy armor we carry so that we can be free to move? To filter the dregs from the wine of our lives so that the world can be a more celebratory place? The same with the trees that bear no fruit: God will trim the trees in our lives that are not offering fruit so that we don't waste our energy, anxiety, time, nutrients, and resources on ways that are not life-giving.

You are not chaff; you have some. Your coworker that drives you crazy is not a fruitless tree; they have some fruitless branches. John has a vision of one who can love the hard-to-find kernels of wheat and take care of the chaff we often hide in for our own sakes. And that is what John the Baptist offers us: ending or exchanging chaff habits for wheat ones. We don't burn to suffer, but to refine. Why do we need fruit in the first place? Because the world is hungry. Where do you want to share more? Where could you use more life in this journey through Luke?

10

Belovedness

Luke 3:21–22

"B aptism" is a transliteration of the Greek word βαπτιζω. "Baptism" is translated as dipping, dyeing, saturating, immersing. John the Dunker officially became John the Baptist in 1611, when the Authorized Version of the King James Bible was, well, authorized. The translators at the time of King James were trying to render the best possible vernacular translation of the Bible and consulted the oldest Hebrew, Greek, and Latin manuscripts available to them, the oldest coming from the late 1200s CE. It was a phenomenal undertaking for its time, ecumenical and even interfaith. But baptism was transliterated, each Greek letter matched to a phonetic English equivalent, instead of translated, because of the tradition of church practice.

For the first three centuries of Christianity, baptism was done by full submersion for adults only, preferably in running water. Baptismal candidates were assigned mentors for a two-year or longer period called the catechumenate. Only if the candidates, the catechumens, proved worthy of the Christian life in their faith and practice could they be baptized and accepted fully into the Christian community. Baptism was thought to cleanse the candidate of sin. As a result, there was a trend to be baptized as late as possible in life so that one might die in a state of grace. The first Christian emperor, Constantine, was baptized on his death bed, some twelve years after presiding over the council that produced the Nicene Creed.

Augustine of Hippo changed this earliest tradition, perhaps unintentionally. Augustine reasoned that baptism did indeed cleanse the candidate of sin, but of a different quality than his forebears had contemplated. Augustine believed that when Adam ate the forbidden fruit, he committed the first, the Original Sin, of pride and disobedience; humanity lost the image of God and passed this fallen nature on genetically, literally through "shriveled sperm." Babies, since the time of Adam, were all born sinners. Baptism removed Original Sin and freed infants from eternal damnation, for Original Sin was, thought Augustine, punishable by hell. By the mid-400s CE, babies were baptized as a result. With infant mortality rates as high as 50 percent, what parent would take a risk on the eternal destiny of their progeny? Immersing a baby increases the likelihood of mortality, so sprinkling became the preferred means of baptism from that point onward.

Curiously enough, around this time theologians began to wonder about whether Mary was a vessel tainted by Original Sin; the Church ultimately decided that she was conceived without it—an Immaculate Conception. This would allow Jesus to have been born without Original Sin, as Joseph did not pass on the "sin gene" and Mary was herself free of it as well. The King James translation was not prepared to question the traditions and rituals in the face of Reformation groups like the Anabaptists, Diggers, and Quakers.

Jesus was like us in every way, but without sin, yet approached John for a baptism of repentance for the forgiveness of sins. Why would Jesus want to be baptized? Maybe he saw a turning point, for himself and for all who choose to walk together toward a larger life, toward the family of God. Afterwards, the veil between heaven and earth was parted, air/breath/wind (Spirit) filled him, and he heard the voice of God say that he was beloved.

Perhaps this voice in Luke and this vision of the Spirit's indwelling is meant to secure our knowledge of his divinity. It could also be the moment when the human Jesus realized that there was nothing he could do to make God love him any less, and nothing he could do to make God love him any more. God's love became secure and out of his control; it changed his life. Luke offers us an invitation. If baptism signifies the unconditional love and acceptance of God, maybe it is heartwarming that most of us cannot remember our own, that we are loved by God from before memory is even possible. Maybe the repentance that Jesus modeled could be our own: no need to hustle for worthiness in the kingdom of God or rack up gems for our spiritual crown. Baptism strips away any belief we trust more fundamentally than we trust God: that we can earn blessings instead of receiving them; that grace as a gift requires something of us; that God is too transcendent, too ephemeral and holy for our filthy rags of righteousness.

In Acts of the Apostles, we are going to meet folks who received the water baptism without the indwelling of the Spirit, without the second wind that comes from God. I was baptized with water at ten years old and I can most certainly tell you that Spirit came later for me and did not seem to be once for all. I am still trying to grow into the baptism of the Spirit, sometimes sneaking little breaths here and there, sometimes coughing from a life so new and big that it is hard for me to hold in. My yoga teacher tells us from time to time that yoga is a breathing class, not an exercise class. Maybe Luke is calling us to a breathing regimen instead of a spiritual exercise?

23andWe

Luke 3:23–38

Luke's genealogy is radically different from Matthew's and, with just a little bit of patience, reveals Luke's unique understanding of Jesus, where he came from, what he came to do, and how we might be invited to follow. Matthew traces Jesus back to Abraham and does so with apparent emphasis on numeric symmetry: the number of generations between Abraham and David is equal to the generations between David and the Babylonian exile is equal to the number of generations from exile until Joseph—14. Fourteen generations symmetrically circumscribe three huge epochs in the history of Israel that had asymmetric spans. Matthew does not present an accurate genealogy, but a symbolic one. Interestingly, it is Matthew that includes women—Tamar, Rahab, and Ruth—and not Luke. Matthew, likely writing to a Jewish audience, mentions Canaanite women in a patriarchal line, each of whom came to faith in the Hebrew God later in life and was praised for their off-color piety. Jesus is, for Matthew, the fulfilment of God's covenant with Abraham, a significant three journeys away, and, though from Abraham and his descendants, open to including those with intentional faith.

Luke, on the other hand, traces the line of Jesus back further than Matthew, going even to Adam, the progenitor of all; Luke identifies Adam as the child of God. Luke seems to be making the claim that Jesus is not only the fulfilment of the Jewish covenant, but of God's creation and care for humanity itself. Jesus is related to Adam. So are the Jews, Greeks, Parthians, Romans, et al. So am I. So are you. Jesus appears as a common member with us in God's household, definitely a Lukan theme and one to continue to grow into: Jesus, and therefore God, cares for humanity as a relative, not just Jews, Christians, or any other limited category.

Luke departs from Matthew not only in the number and pattern of ancestors, eschewing the three cycles of fourteen that Matthew high-lights, but even differs on the forebears themselves, perhaps most signifi-cantly after David. Matthew links Jesus to David through Solomon; Luke through Nathan. While it is possible that Nathan was one of Solomon's many nicknames ("Jedidiah" was certainly one), David did have another son named Nathan, whose lineage seems lost to us today. Perhaps, how-ever, Luke is not tracing Jesus's link through David through Nathan, but rather referring to a nonbiological character in the David story, Nathan the prophet. After David steals Bathsheba—the wife of his bodyguard Uriah the Hittite—learns of her pregnancy, and kills her husband, Nathan the prophet confronts David, getting him to condemn himself through an ana-logical tale about a rich man who steals a poor man's sheep. Nathan will not only serve to convict the Davidic conscience, but later anoints David's successful successor, Solomon, as the new king. Perhaps Luke is trying to link Jesus not only to David and the Hebrew Golden Age, but also to repentance, to challenging unqualified power, to speaking truth when the emperor is naked. Jesus certainly does all of these things in Luke, and per-haps a reminder for us, still relatively early in Luke, is to join our relative, Jesus, in unmasking abuses of power. As G. K. Chesterton once observed, "Men [people] do not differ much about what things they will call evils; they differ enormously about what evils they will call excusable."[4] What evils do we settle for in our business, home, and national lives that God might be asking us, as relatives of both Jesus and Nathan, to unmask and repent of?

4. Gilber Keith Chesterton *The Collected Works of G.K. Chesterton: The Illustrated London News, 1908–1910* (San Francisco, CA: Ignatius Press, 1986). 413.

Finally, both Luke and Matthew go out of their way to make the reader know that Joseph was not the biological father of Jesus, but both Gospels recount Jesus's genealogy through Joseph; Joseph is the relative to David, not Mary, and therefore Jesus is not actually related to David. This might help my thoughts on Nathan the prophet make more sense; Jesus resonates with David as he will unite the scattered and offer a new way of living, a way that exceeds even what David could imagine. Jesus's importance is so much greater than biology, but fulfills an icon. It reminds us, perhaps, that whenever we get bogged down on facts in these stories instead of how God might be asking us to reconsider our lives, our neighbors, and God, we might be missing an opportunity. We also have an opportunity as we read the Gospel to reflect on how Jesus fulfills scripture—he brings alive old stories in new, powerful ways.

12

Resistance

Luke 4:1–14

Just as John proclaimed God's saving presence in the desert, can Jesus hold his new vision, breath, and trust in God? Fresh from his second wind, driven by the Spirit into the desert, Jesus is put to the test. The devil shows up for the first time (Greek διαβολος, *diabolos*). Once again, tradition has turned a transliteration into a title. *Diabolos* means "slanderer" or "one who throws so much as to throw through," seated in accusation. *Satan* is similar: "accuser." In the Hebrew Bible, there is no personal force of evil opposed to God. The serpent in the Garden of Eden is not Lucifer ("light-bearer") and "old Slew" does not possess the Egyptian pharaoh to resist God.

Everything in the Hebrew Bible comes from God—Pharaoh hardens his own heart and then God does. God torments Saul with an evil spirit. "Satan" does not appear in Job, but "the accuser" does, a superhuman being who is likely best understood as God's chief prosecutor / district attorney. This accuser asks God about Job; God permits Job's trials. People didn't get really creative with the discomfort of these vignettes until after the Bible had already been written. Their discomfort culminated in Dante's *Inferno* and Milton's *Paradise Lost*, both of which have shaped the Christian view of the spiritual world more than the Bible has. The Bible names an accuser, a slanderer, a voice of doubt or shame or fear. Maybe these voices are evil, but more likely, they are natural.

Jewish tradition does not include a personal figure of evil; instead, there is the *yetzer harah*, a spirit that tempts people to settle for the good instead of the better, to be less than they are. Resisting the *yetzer harah* pushes people beyond the comfortable, bringing joy and life to the world, refining themselves. The temptations of Jesus might make a great deal more sense if we understand the tempter this way, rather than as a devil figure who is clearly subordinate to God trying to goad Jesus into skydiving without a parachute.

Jesus has gone to meditate and learn a new way of breathing, a new way of being. He gives up food for a really long time—forty days. This is possible, though pretty excruciating. Luke seems to be trying to get the reader to connect the number forty with its biblical representation instead of its physical challenges, however. Forty is a symbolic number in the Bible: rain for forty days flooded the world, but Noah and the animals were safe in the ark. After forty days, the world started over, cleaned from the blood of Abel and the violence of the human heart. Forty years of wandering in the desert after the Exodus to grow dependent on God, during which time the people ate manna from heaven. The Torah recounts that people were not ready to enter the Promised Land after the Exodus, because they would have had to subdue the Canaanites already living there and they were afraid. It took forty years for them to make a journey of just over forty days. The time was not wasted; it was needed for them to live into God's gift. Jesus takes his time to start over, to be a new person, to grow in his trust of God.

The slanderer shows up and asks Jesus to make bread for himself. Nothing sinful about that. How could it be tempting? Many Jewish people at the time of Jesus believed that God would send them a deliverer from Roman tyranny, a leader who would help the Jewish people become self-governing and relive the Golden Age of King David. The Messiah would end hunger for a people living on the edge of famine, present himself with glory in the temple, and vanquish infidels, heretics, pagans, and political enemies with military might and cunning. The Messiah they asked for was a king of kings. If Jesus could turn stones into bread, he could easily supply a food-strapped people. The Messiah they expected would present himself (they definitely expected a male figure) in a supernatural way at the temple in Jerusalem (some modern Jews have massaged this to expect the Messiah to either rebuild or to usher a third temple from heaven). What could be more dramatic than jumping off the peak of the temple before an estimated 4 million worshippers during Passover week and floating safely to the ground? All Jesus would have to do is accept the lie that what other people wanted from him is what God wanted, that Jesus needed to hustle for merit in God's eye.

We don't live by bread alone. Our ancestors in the wilderness were fed by God, but they died. In fact, the book of Numbers insinuates that the forty years in the desert were so the nonbelieving recipients of the Exodus could die and God could start over with their descendants, inviting a new generation toward faith and larger life. Abraham Maslow, an American psychologist of the twentieth century, reminds us that reliable food is essential for us to consider education and philosophy, but bread is the foundation for larger life, not its limitation.

How much of my time I waste worrying about whether a natural expression of myself will be well received! As if I could control what someone else receives. Jesus might just decide to follow God's light even if no one else does, even if it leads to spending time with outcasts and sinners, even if it leads him to love himself, pimples on prom night and all. The slanderer (remember, slander is the crime of making a false statement with the intent to damage someone's reputation) defames not only Jesus, but God, quoting scripture to incite Jesus to do something against his faith. If you jump and God saves you, you will know God loves you. If you pray and get what you want, you will know you are worthy. Jesus declines testing an answer, he has already decided to park his trust in God during his time in the desert —no need to test God; he is already loved as he is. Jesus resists. The slanderer retires. He'll come back. At inopportune times, worry, shame, and accusation always seem to coax us into being less than God intends for us.

We could read this story as a caution against insidious accusations about our worth before God, temptations of works righteousness, and transactional approaches to God and each other. Jesus models that we can resist the *yetzer harah*. Maybe we need to look at these temptations and say, I do want that, but only to validate myself, and God has already justified my existence. Do I quote the scriptures to justify what I already think and to say God hates the same people or parts of myself that I do, or am I willing to recalibrate my aim? Do I slander my neighbor and myself, or do I live into the truth of being God's beloved?

Observance

Luke 4:16–21

At the time of Jesus, Sadducees held that only the Torah counted as Holy Scripture (Genesis, Exodus, Leviticus, Numbers, and Deuteronomy). Sadducees were primarily concerned with ritual observance of the Torah, particularly cultic ritual and temple sacrifice. They were both socially and religiously conservative, believing that as God had already said all there was to say and there was no resurrection of the dead. Sadducees controlled the temple and the priesthood; they had a strong working relationship with Rome, helping store taxation documents in the temple and collecting taxes.

Pharisees, though often slammed in the Gospels, believed that God cared about ethical and moral observations of God's law in addition to temple and cultic observations. Pharisees believed that God had spoken beyond the Torah, through the prophets, psalms, and other writings. Some Pharisees believed in a resurrection of the dead; all believed in right action of believers on behalf of the community. Pharisees tithed of all their goods, instead of only the ones prescribed in the Torah, to make up for the Jews who did not. Pharisees fasted each week to make up for the Jews who did not fast on the one mandated day of the year, Yom Kippur. Pharisees were the ones you would expect help from when you got a flat tire or were caught up short on your light bill. Pharisees shared the concerns of the

Sadducees for cultic practice, but also sought ways for God to influence their daily life and interactions.

Zealots were freedom fighters, ancient Zionists, who believed religiously in a Jewish state. Some were guerillas, some were assassins, particularly a group called the Sicarrii, which means "long knife." Sicarrii were ancient-day terrorists who would assassinate Roman soldiers in large crowds and then slip away. Difficult to catch or identify, they took the fun out of soldiering in Judea. It is likely that Judas Iscariot was a Sicarrii. Another disciple, Simon the Zealot, was certainly a freedom fighter. With Matthew as a tax collector, it is helpful and hopeful to know that at least a few of Jesus's original disciples categorically hated one another.

Essenes, who most scholars credit as curators of the Dead Sea Scrolls, believed that most Jewish people were lax in their religious discipline and did not practice enough holiness. They separated themselves from the temple, which they believed was defiled, and lived near the Dead Sea in the desert, where every member practiced on a daily basis the holiness required only of priests and only on high holy days: they were celibate, immersed themselves seven times a day to cleanse ritual contaminants, and wore only linen garments. Essenes seem to have contributed to our later personification of the devil by calling their fellow Jews (and not the pagan Romans) "children of darkness" while reserving "children of the light" for themselves.

Jesus's first sermon offers several insights into his personhood and guidance into our own. His Pharisaic upbringing shows when he chooses not to read from the Torah, but from Isaiah, stressing that God cares deeply about our everyday decisions. Jesus believed that God is still speaking; we are invited to listen for God's voice today and follow it by the way we treat our lives and our neighbors.

Jesus picks as his first reading a lovely text that really describes the Jubilee year. Once a week on the Sabbath, God's people were to rest from their work so they could recuperate and enjoy not only one another, but God's presence in time itself. To safeguard this practice, rules limiting work were adopted so that no one would spend the Sabbath washing dishes or catching up on work, allowing the ability to rest. These laws were meant to protect the intent of the Sabbath by proscribing distractions. Every Sabbath year (one in seven) there were other imperatives, including resting the land so that its minerals could recuperate and not be overfarmed.

Every seven seven-years, the fiftieth year, was a Jubilee year—a Sabbath of Sabbaths. The Jubilee saw total debt forgiveness so that slavery would not be a perpetual inheritance. Lands taken in default were restored. We do not know whether the Jubilee was ever practiced, but it is certainly described in the Torah. "The year of the Lord's favor" is most certainly Isaiah's reference to a Jubilee of Jubilees, one in which not only lands and freedom are restored, but also sight. In his first public speaking in the temple, Jesus announces the fulfillment of the Jubilee.

We don't know whether this occurred in a Jubilee year and it is doubtful that the folks listening in the synagogue ripped up their debt records then and there. What does Jesus mean, then? Perhaps that God's intention for levelling the low places is not on a fifty-year cycle, but a constant invitation for us to practice. Perhaps Jesus challenged the practice of waiting every fifty years for real forgiveness and second chances, when the opportunity is at hand immediately! If discipleship is about living larger, why should we only try it once a year during Lent or on New Year's instead of once a day/hour/second? Jesus knows God wants more for the world and he intends to do something about it. Maybe Jesus isn't preaching to the crowd, but making a sacred decision in their presence.

14

Radical Vision

Luke 4:22–30

Many scholars think the crowd will get angry at Jesus because he leaves out the next phrase of Isaiah "and to proclaim the day of vengeance of our God." These scholars believe that Isaiah wrote revenge into the Jubilee of Jubilees and that popular enjoyment of Isaiah 61 was predicated on vengeance over enemies, including Rome. This may be true, but I invite your reading of Isaiah 61 anew. There is no description of God's vengeance that involves any punishing of enemies or violence, only the restoration of the poor, the healing of the ill, the dissolution of shame. And what if Jesus realizes that God's vengeance, so unlike our own, is forgiveness? Revenge, for us, is never really about getting even; it is about inflicting someone else with pain because we have suffered. Getting even is about receiving our defrauded goods back with appropriate interest. Getting revenge is about humiliating, charging usurious interest, defaming, or damaging. What if Jesus has made the public decision that since we are all members of God's family, it will be really awkward for us to live pettily, as we will have to see one another again at the next family function? What if he has decided that God's Jubilee of Jubilees only waits for us and that we should not make God wait? What if God asked us to give up vengeance as revenge for Luke? For Lent?

For life? What if vengeance as forgiveness and restoration are the garments of salvation we are invited to wear each and every day?

Jesus is like the guy who goes to an Ivy League college from small town America and comes back the pride of the town. Or the youth group kid that was so remarkably pleasant to be around who goes off to seminary and comes back suddenly concerned with social justice to everyone else's consternation. One of my own family members was grievously disappointed in my decision to attend seminary and told me that seminaries ruin good faith and proper preaching. Perhaps this is exactly the crowd Jesus encounters. After all, they taught him what to believe throughout his developing life, so who was he to imply that they'd missed something? Was he biting the hands that fed him? Self-righteous and pompous? He should be thanking them for their gifts of mentorship and using his miracle-working powers for them first as they had been his godparents.

Jesus perceives that the hometown crowd expects his allegiance and thanks, instead of his reflections and growth. He references miracles in Capernaum that Luke does not describe. He then gives them some tough love. He recounts how the prophets of old did their most fabulous miracles in the lands of Canaanite pagans. Elijah helped a Canaanite widow, a poor lady of a different ethnicity and likely different religion. That's like helping a Muslim lady in the Bible Belt or a good Christian lady in Saudi Arabia.

It could be that Jesus is full of teen spirit, oppositional like a rebel with only minor cause. Or it could be that Jesus realized that the Jubilee of Jubilees is not just for some, but an invitation into a radical vision for all. If this is the case, then Jesus might actually be read as trusting that those who knew him as a child and adolescent are capable of hearing his insight and changing. Perhaps he does not criticize to break down, shame, or challenge because he already has a relationship with his audience, trusts and cares enough about them to see them grow, to build up, to transform. If this is the case, perhaps he is modeling some boundary setting for us. Brené Brown notes that we ought to choose the discomfort of setting meaningful boundaries over the inevitable resentment that comes when we do not.[5] Do we often wait to express our hurt, anger, or disappointment until we are hurt or angry? Beyond challenging the limits of our grace by including outsiders, maybe Jesus is also inviting us to offer and receive feedback lovingly with the expectation of transformation instead of reacting in punitive terms, to guide us out of resentment.

Try two possible practices today: (1) Hear a criticism as an invitation to change because the critic believes you can and wants to enjoy their relationship with you even more, instead of condemnation. (2) Offer a criticism from this vantage point instead of fearing the boundary. Extra credit: imagine God loving someone you do not, cannot, or will not love until the seed of radical love takes root in you; allow Jesus to walk through your midst as you follow him on his Way.

---

5. Brené Brown. *The Gifts of Imperfection: Let Go of Who You Think You're Supposed to Be and Embrace Who You Are* (Center City, MN: Hazelden, 2010), 33.

15

Unclean Spirits

Luke 4:31–37

Demon (δαεμον) is a transliteration from Greek, meaning "unclean spirit." Folk legends about evil powers are not biblical and can definitely interfere with how we understand Jesus's mission and ministry, along with our own. Demonology describes evil insidious spirits that plot with Satan to thwart God and steal souls for hell. If this is not what the New Testament describes, then what is a demon, an "unclean spirit"? The term is often applied to abnormal and (apparently) irreformable behaviors and personalities.

Today we understand more about the human psyche, including addiction, such as how chemical structures in the brain are altered by alcohol and narcotics. Healthy people who become addicted to a substance or behavior can exhibit a radical change of behavior, including neglect of responsibilities. Something has changed in their functioning at a level as fundamental as breathing.

Victims of abuse and neglect can also become disconnected from society. They often suffer from a fundamental challenge to trust in the goodness of the universe, the reliability of others, and imputation of any inherent value in themselves. Today we also recognize numerous psychological conditions and although the diagnostic tools are in place, the remedies are not. Abuse victims *are* victims. They may have "unclean

43

spirits," but they didn't earn or deserve them. In the mideighties, people with AIDS were ostracized; they were often viewed as morally depraved, receiving a just punishment. We were afraid and we vilified not only the germs, but the people as unclean.

The man who speaks to Jesus might have had schizophrenia, Tourette's syndrome, or autism. Whatever his medical condition, people were afraid of him. One wonders if he was even allowed to speak to anyone, or if Jesus was the first person to listen. At first glance, it appears Jesus silences the man, but Jesus might rather silence the stigma that separated the man from his community, especially on the Sabbath and in the synagogue.

Jesus might be calling us to a community in which the clean and the unclean are united in God's family, where people are not expelled because they do not fit the norms. Is Jesus implying that people label and dehumanize one another? What if the unclean spirit he drove out that day was the fear, blame, and prejudice of everyone else against the man? What if what he offered was the community that is necessary for all of us? He works this miracle in the middle of a religious service on the Sabbath to remind us what the Sabbath is for—to serve humanity—and how we honor God by loving those in front of us, no matter how distracting or scary it can be.

Each week in Episcopal churches we pass the Peace, and most often just say hi. The Peace was, however, designed to be a time and a space for the estranged to be reconciled, for confession and absolution to happen in God's presence before the Eucharist. Peace and reconciliation are built into our liturgical history, but might profit from a little more investment in our present. Who do you need to reconcile with? Are there people who show up as unclean for you? What would it take to be in community with them? Instead of them changing, could you?

16

Blessed to Bless

Luke 4:38–41

Hardwired into every Southerner, and even more so at the time of Jesus, is the notion of hospitality, of showing honor to guests and family members. Staying at a hotel when visiting relatives would be a double slight, as would not eating at a family meal. The host's vocation, not just their job, is to provide for their guests. There is something deeply gratifying about creating the space for conversation and time together by seeing to the atmosphere, cleaning, cooking, and serving, and also in pouring one's time, thoughts, and self into such occasions. Due to her illness, Simon's mother-in law is unable to do this. We could take this story at face value, viewing Jesus's healing as a means to help her meet her cultural expectations. We could also read this as Jesus removing a roadblock for her to serve a meaningful role in the community by providing for conversations, connections, and enjoyment of life.

It is interesting to think about this even more broadly: Simon's mother-in-law is nourished by Jesus and then uses the energy she has been given in mission. When God calls Abraham (Gen. 12) to leave his family and home and travel to a promised land he has never seen and cannot imagine, God is very clear: I will bless you to be a blessing; all the peoples of the earth will be blessed by you. Abraham is not given luxuries to bask in; he is nourished by God so that he can expend this holy energy in serving others.

Abraham is a sort of satellite, helping folks find the richness of God's grace that sometimes struggle with the signal. He is not a baron in the kingdom of God, he is a butler in the family of God. So is Simon's mother-in-law. So are we. God's blessings are not for hoarding, but for enriching the world. Simon's mother-in-law might ask us to consider not only what our blessings are, but why God shares them with us and how we can join God in sharing our blessings with others.

Luke doesn't stop here. Jesus continues to heal others as the word spreads of what he has done. As in the previous chapter, the unclean spirits seem to better understand Jesus than the clean folks, the disciples, the priests, and Pharisees. The demons know he is favored by God; they know that Jesus is able to remove the additional barriers to community that we create for the sick, suffering, and different. Jesus is able to silence the objections of these unclean spirits that lobby self-destructively for division and threaten to isolate and destroy the creatures of God. This is the work of the children of God.

Jesus lives into the use of power that God intends: he is blessed to be a blessing. We can too. We are much richer than Jesus ever was, much more educated. We have greater access to nutrition and networks. God hopes that we will use this access, these blessings, to be a blessing to others, especially to those who suffer from the divisiveness of the unclean spirits.

There is something worth noticing through Luke about how ordinary all of these people and interactions are. Jesus heals a lady so she can serve the small dinner party she'd planned. Simon (Peter) is married. The next reading in chapter 17 will show that he is mediocre at his job. And that's the point. God is not worried we will lose a sense of awe and wonder in resplendence, but that we have lost awe and wonder in the ordinary. We might just find that what is ordinary is a blessing, and then use this profound insight to be ordinary blessings ourselves.

17

Go Fish

Luke 4:42–5:11

In the previous chapter we read that Jesus healed Simon's mother-in-law. In this reading, he commandeers Simon's fishing boat, gives unsolicited fishing advice, and then gives Simon a vocational opportunity. Jesus must have known this guy for some time, eating at his mother-in-law's house and hanging around with the fisherfolk. Maybe Jesus was a regular supply preacher in the area. Maybe Simon's mother-in-law had the best fried chicken.

Notice how the crowds search for Jesus, even looking in deserted places, and upon finding him, they try and keep him for themselves (hoarding blessings instead of living into them by sharing). Jesus offers a polite rebuke, but the message is clear: God is interested in everyone getting the message that life is too short to settle for cheap and broken ways of living. Glad you all appreciate the message, so let's share it with the world.

Jesus goes looking for space, twice. Once in a deserted place, the other in a boat. The first time he is by himself, the second instance he's looking to escape the pressure of his peers, so that he can actually communicate with them.

He sees some guys he has met before. They have been fishing all night, the best time for fishing. They are professional fishermen. They have failed at their jobs by catching nothing all night. Jesus has an idea for them. Jesus, the landlubber. The carpenter. Has a fishing idea. Go out further and throw your nets (in the middle of the day!) into the deep waters. One wonders whether they did this against their own instincts, expecting to fail just so they could come back and put Jesus in his place for not knowing how to fish. They go through the motions and then realize the guy they'd met was offering something different than they had heard from him in the past. Their catch is so large that Simon Peter asks Jesus to leave. Peter isn't worthy; he is a sinful man.

"Deep water" is an interesting phrase. It could, of course, be a literal phrase that describes depth and topography. Water is a symbol of chaos in the Bible, and deep water would be deep chaos—a place where the unclean spirits are free to roam, where curfew is 5:00 p.m. with bars on all windows and doors. "Go there," says Jesus, "and cast your nets." And not just any old net. Bishop Andy Doyle has offered that the net Jesus refers to here is a drag net, not a surface cast.[6] Drag nets catch all kinds of things— fish, tires, boots—desirables and undesirables. Jesus wants even the undesirables drawn out of the chaos. Is Simon worried about his worthiness? Is he concerned that his love is too narrow or too shallow for what Jesus has in mind? But Jesus does not go away. He stubbornly ups the ante and says, "Now you will catch people, desirable and undesirable alike."

How do you fish for people? Analogies can be really helpful guides to figuring out something we are unfamiliar with. But they can also be held so tightly that all the insight they offer is squeezed out of them. Do we fish with bait-and-switch pizza parties that trick people into loving Jesus? Do we try to convert hungry people stuck at laundromats with intellectual arguments about "good news" they may not perceive as anything good?

Perhaps Jesus is upping the ante in suggesting that we fish for people by being fish. Swim in a way that is compelling. Swim in a community that holds us and others up. Communities of fish allow for drafting, rotation of leadership, healing, pooling resources. Communities of fish let the

---

6. Andy Doyle, "Epiphany 5C," Hitchhiking the World, February 2, 2019, http://hitchhikingthebible.blogspot.com/2019/02/epiphany-5c-february-10-2019-under.html.

injured rest inside the school. They scare away predators. They learn to be in sync with one another's needs. Communities of faith scare unclean spirits. They are places of healing and support. But we have to play our part. Jesus compels us to welcome in some that might not make our cut—fish that were drag-netted by God's standards, not ours.

Be a fish. Nothing more. Nothing less. Be aware of the selfishness of every motive. Be awkward. Be drawn to Jesus. Draw undesirable people and the undesirable parts of ourselves from the deep chaos into his presence. Jesus's disciples are afraid he will judge them as so many others have done. Jesus wants to catch the people and pieces of our lives in the deep chaos. And he wants us to help.

18

Catching the Cooties

Luke 5:12–16

In the Bible, "leprosy" is a catch-all for any abnormal skin condition that could be contagious, dangerous, or just gross: innocuous rashes, athlete's foot, hives, cold sores, or chigger bites, gangrene, impetigo, ringworm. Having any type of abnormality made one unclean. The ideal person was blemish free, just as a lamb without blemish, without stripes, spots, or missing wool was worthy to be sacrificed to God. High priests could not have scars and serve. There is evidence that disliked high priests had their earlobes slashed in the marketplace, effectively ending their careers by vandalizing their pristine bodies.

"Uncleanliness" was not a bacterial designation, but a ritual term, sort of like the cooties from the playgrounds of my childhood. Once you get the cooties, there is no way to remove them. You are an agent of infection until the game is over. In Jesus's time this "game" never ended and was played not only by kids, but adults and adults with power. What if the cooties were actually dangerous to your family, village, and soul? What if you could get them not only through obvious contact, like tag, but by touching someone who appeared to be clean, eating meat that you thought was fully kosher, being touched by the shadow of an infected person?

To remove the vestiges of unclean contagions, some folks took ritual baths in *mikvahs*, some as often as five times a day. These baths were fed by "living waters," which really meant moving water, including rain, rivers, streams. The hope was any unintentionally contracted uncleanliness would be washed off. But what if it did not?

Being unclean led to direct physical punishment for fear of spreading leprosy and famine in the village. In this story from Luke, the man with the skin condition was ostracized and even denounced. He could have earned his disease by intentionally courting it or not engaging in the proper cleansing rituals. He got what he deserved and was an advertisement to the community every day to be vigilant.

But he asks Jesus, if he is willing, to make him clean. What an interesting question. Was Jesus surprised? We have seen Jesus deal with unclean spirits, but blemished bodies? Maybe Jesus had not considered this option at all, but he responds, "Well, now that you ask, I am willing, so be clean." The rash, hives, birthmark, Hepatitis C clears up and the man can no longer be shunned. Jesus then tells him to go to the priest and publicly get the needed blessing. The mark is benign, not malignant. The man is restored to the community.

The crowds want Jesus to take care of their dis-eases. Perfectionism? Alcohol abuse? Shame? Fear of disappointing our families/parents/kids/coworkers? Jesus withdraws, perhaps to be refreshed, but also to offer us the opportunity to do this work with him and not simply expect God to take care of it for us.

Public health and serious illness are important. However, do we cast people out for fear they are contagious when they really have a social shame, be it bankruptcy, a misdemeanor, or a tattoo? Maybe we cannot work the miracle of removing a physical mark, but perhaps we can make people clean by risking exposure for the sake of community. Will someone's poor fiscal management rub off on you? Will their dyed hair threaten your own image? Will our fear isolate and destroy creatures of God or can we make the unclean clean by our love and presence? How can we heal and be healed?

19

Friendship

Luke 5:17–26

The man on the mat, undoubtedly paralyzed because of his sins or unworthiness, has no agency whatsoever. Paralyzed, he cannot come to Jesus on his own. He cannot resist his friends trying to bring him to Jesus. He may have been screaming at the top of his lungs for these friends to put him down. We don't know. We do know that the friends were brazen enough to not only bring him to Jesus, but to overcome obstacles. A la *Mission Impossible*, they persevere and cut a hole in someone's roof. They destroy someone's property. They do whatever it takes to get their friend to Jesus. Jesus commends their faith, not the paralyzed guy. Their faith is enough. Enough to get his sins forgiven. Their friend walks away.

Remember, people assumed he was paralyzed because he had sinned. If he could walk, the sin was gone. How can Jesus forgive sins? When Jesus asks which is harder to do—forgive sins or tell someone to walk—he is really saying that both are equally hard and he has done them both.

We've previously read about breaking taboos to love "unclean" people, but now Luke and Jesus challenge us to be the kind of friends that love people into larger life, even if they go kicking and screaming. Jesus is challenging us to be persistent friends, to avoid giving up on each other because of different paralyses that make walking in faith together difficult, to avoid saying "We all make our own decisions, so who am I to offer advice?"; to stop making only "I" statements and think about "us."

The Nicene Creed begins, "We believe." I am not sure that my soul resonates deeply with the Creed every time I say it, but I am convinced that someone in the congregation does, so together *we* believe. On those days of doubt, numbness, or just mental haze, my friends carry me and I pray I will get to return the favor. We believe. My paralysis is carried. *We* believe. Jesus invites us into being with the paralyzed as we journey in faith together. Who is your "we" today? Who is offering to carry you further? How might you enjoy the ride instead of resisting it? Who might you support in faith?

It is true that God alone can forgive sins, but it is equally true that we rarely live into God's forgiveness as a community or individually, by breaking down the barriers of isolation that sin so often leaves behind. Jesus invites us to walk out of our paralysis, to bring others to God, confident that God can restore our communities and that God believes in our inherent worthiness. Jesus tells us that faithful friends do not leave one another paralyzed in shame or fear or resignation, but calls us to move together in faith, helping others on their way and receiving help ourselves.

20

New Wineskins

Luke 5:27–39

Jesus made friends, students, and disciples of a diverse group of folks who had reason to hate one another. Matthew was a tax collector, Simon a Zealot, and Judas possibly a mega-Zealot Sicarrii. Jesus kept them from killing each other, kept them together, and knit them into a community that has outlived him by nearly two thousand years, to date. The twelve disciples, as well as the earliest churches, had radically different political, theological, and moral views. Their differences of opinion may not have changed, but how they responded to each other did, with Jesus beside them.

I grew up in churches that were pretty homogeneous racially, socio-economically, theologically, and doctrinally. I could offer a question, but had to be careful not to ask radical questions. We were loved as we were, unless we thought "b" instead of "a" or doubted the doctrines of the community. We could not risk questioning certain things, such as why couldn't divorced persons be deacons or women ministers, because to do so would be an affront to the Bible, to Jesus, or God. God could not tolerate our doubts because God could not tolerate our differences.

Jesus not only tolerated differences in his disciples, he called them in their differences. He did not fear the things that often terrify us. What if we trusted God enough to make difference central to our identity as people of God instead of a threat to it? What if we loved folks enough to listen deeply, to love them not in spite of their theology or politics, but because of them, even if our own do not change? What if churches were encouraged to be communities where difference is appreciated and not feared? We need new wineskins for this holy work.

Jean Piaget, a Swiss psychologist, developed a learning theory more than one hundred years ago that seems all about old garments and new wineskins. According to Piaget, we have a worldview, no matter how simple or flawed, that works until we encounter new information that does not match our worldview. We then have a crisis: Will we change our worldview to accommodate the new information, or will we dismiss the information by assimilating it into our preconceived notions?

Our faith leaks when we try to assimilate the gospel into the worldview of our cultural values and present opinions. The gospel cannot be stitched into our lives like a patch; it requires us to radically accommodate our habits, values, and practices around God's good news. Adding a little will not satisfy; it will cheapen both our lives and the gospel. We need a new container for new contents that can stretch and grow with God; a new garment instead of a fragile and threadbare one that will easily tear.

What if God is asking us to give up what we have been in order to make room for where God would like to take us, a place that will be better and more enjoyable for us? Can we trust and follow God? Can we be worthy containers of God's wine for the world?

And what if God's wine seems like dregs to us? How do we acquire a taste for grace that can seem so, well, distasteful at first sip? I remember how long it took my Baptist-formed palette of juice alone to take communion wine without desperately wanting to spit it out. I am well converted now, so much so that I can't understand why people do not enjoy wine as I now do. Maybe we show up and drink from God's cup and ask for our tastes to change to the One who offers us ever-new wine? Maybe we stretch and grow into discipleship by showing up with tax collectors and Tea Party members and Yellow Dog Democrats to celebrate God's grace together, not in denial of, but in full recognition of our differences. And if we drink from the same cup long enough, may God help us enjoy it and one another wherever Jesus is both our host and our guest.

21

The Sabbath

Luke 6:1–10

Shabbat begins on Friday after sunset, when three stars are visible in the sky. *Shabbat* comes from the Hebrew number seven. A Jewish idiom says more than the Jews have kept the Sabbath, the Sabbath has kept the Jews. At this meal, the oldest woman in the home lets her hair down from the *sheitel* that may have covered it all week and lights two candles. The oldest man lifts a goblet filled with wine, the Kiddush cup, blesses it, and offers a share around the table. A third element of Shabbat is the blessing of the bread, typically challah, and matzah within the Passover Festival. The meal is meant to be festive. Travelers are to be invited to a Shabbat meal, even if they do not know the host. The day of rest is not about doing nothing, but minimizing distractions of work and preparation to be fully present with God and one another.

Around the time of Jesus, a group of Jewish leaders wanted to "build a fence around the Torah." The Torah (Genesis, Exodus, Leviticus, Numbers, and Deuteronomy), is the most authoritative among the Hebrew Scriptures in Judaism and considered God's greatest gift, not as laws, but as a guide for living more fully with God and one another. The Jewish leaders were concerned that people who walked the edge of Torah observance might fall off, even by mistake, and miss out on God's gifts. So they tried to build a fence around the Torah to prevent such slips. To protect the Sabbath, the fence defines work very specifically so people do not work by accident.

In this reading from Luke, the Pharisees get upset that the pupils of rabbi Jesus are working on the Sabbath, picking kernels of grain. This is not defined as work in the written Torah, but was agreed on in the oral Torah, handed down from rabbi to rabbi by word of mouth. The disciples should know better, but really the insinuation is that Jesus should know better. Two vignettes unfold about the day of perfection that are deeply rooted in Jewish tradition.

According to Genesis 1, when God begins to create, the earth is messy, chaotic, and covered with water. All the elements are comingled. God begins by making light and there is an evening and a morning. God does not make the sun. God makes light. The result is time itself. Curiously enough, Stephen Hawking agrees that time came first.[7] With light and dark, there can be time. God calls it good. Evening and morning, day one. Then God separates the water from the sky, heaven from earth. God calls it good. Evening and morning, day two. Then God separates the earth from the water and calls for all the plants. God calls it good. Evening and morning, day three. Then God goes through the cycle again, filling the spaces made in the first three days with life and governance. God makes the big light, the lesser light, and then all the other little lights: sun, moon, and stars. Evening and morning, day four. Then God fills the sea and the sky with birds and fish. God calls it good. Evening and morning, day five. God fills the earth with earth-life: all the animals, including people. God calls it good. Evening and morning, day six.

Then, on the Shabbat, the seventh day, God looks at all of Creation and says it is very good. God rests. Notice, however, there is no evening and morning on the seventh day. Where does God rest? The rabbinic answer is time itself. When is the seventh day? The rabbinic answer is that it continues to unfold. How do we keep the Sabbath? By enjoying God's presence in time itself, in all places and acts and peoples. I have a huge beanbag

---

7. Cf. Stephen Hawking, *A Brief History of Time* (New York: Bantam Dell Publishing Group, 1988), chap. 2.

sofa at my home and I love to sprawl out and fill it up with my body. It is not always physically comfortable, but it is restful. God is stretching to fill up time itself with God's presence and we join the Sabbath when we feel God filling us up.

Jesus doesn't say that the Torah should be without fences; he says even the best fences are permeable. He says that the Sabbath is observed by playing with it. God filled time with God's presence for us, not the other way around. We join God's creative enjoyment of the universe when we feed the hungry and when we eat. We join God's creative work when we are still and thankful and when we recognize that God is present not only in moments, but in people. We observe the Sabbath when we wonder at the strength it takes people to carry their burdens instead of judging them for the burdens they carry.

We were created to stretch out into the universe God has given us, to find its inherent "very goodness" even in moments of cognitive dissonance. Fences protect us from defilement, but they also keep us from holiness. Jesus seems to think holiness is worth the risk. What fences do we erect and patrol that keep folks from the very goodness, the holiness of God that yearns to stretch into every moment? What gates and pathways could we join Jesus in building? Not enough time in the day? What if, just for a moment, we could enjoy time itself, unproductive, awkwardly silent, by trusting that God is fully in it and yearns to be fully in us?

22

Blessings and Woes

Luke 6:17–26

The Sermon on the Mount? That's Matthew. Jesus goes up on the mount and gives a several-chapter address that crystallizes the insights of the Torah. Jesus is a new Moses, giving not laws, but guiding God's people into joyful living. Jesus stands on the plain in Luke, a backdrop of topographical equality. Jesus speaks with authority among people, not down to them. Jesus also speaks about how it is that we live as plain folk instead of in a hierarchy of mountain folk.

Blessed are those who mourn? That's an oxymoron if we're talking the way we Southerners use the word "bless." "Bless your heart" can mean you are incapable. Sometimes we hear someone is struggling and we say, "Bless you." God help you. Blessing is complicated, nuanced, and can be dismissive, derisive, or even just a polite way of throwing up our hands. Not here. The word "blessed," *makarios* in Greek and *asher* in Hebrew, is best translated as "joyful." Joyful are those who mourn. Paradoxical, but maybe right. Maybe invulnerable people who never mourn are also impervious to joy. Perhaps when we express sympathy without empathy or compassion, we have immunized ourselves against feeling any emotion, choosing to believe the lie that circumstances dictate the quality of our lives. Blessed are those who choose compassion because life is complex;

even as we mourn with the suffering, we rejoice in compassion and in solidarity itself.

Blessed are the poor. Joyful now. This seems rife for potential abuse. If poor people are happy, then helping them could hurt them. If the poor are blessed, then maybe we get a blessing when we impoverish others. Are the poor blessed because they have fewer choices in the cereal aisle? Too many choices are overwhelming and wouldn't it be nice if we just lived more simply? Maybe. Theirs is the family of God. Now, not when they die. Does God prefer poor people? Does God prefer anyone over another? Matthew calls them "poor in spirit." I'm not sure Luke meant the same thing. Jesus identifies with the prophetic tradition that elevates the poor who are rich in justice and contrition. Being a part of a family that is beyond our choosing involves some work for all of us. We can choose to always be right or we can trade rightness for relationship. Happy are people who make room for others. The more room we make, the more comfort others have to live and breathe and move.

If this is a fair assumption, then the rest makes sense. People who have room in their stomachs and who are hungry for more can be nourished by different fare: by the Eucharist, by diversity, by others. Woe to people who are full because there is no room for God to do anything else in their lives. Woe to people who choose invulnerability over authenticity, who are too full to make room for others, who can't make room for the gifts of imperfection.

There is a Jewish mystical tradition that God made room for the world in God's self at Creation, just as a mother makes room for a child in her own body. Room, in this sense, is not just granting access, but giving nourishment and life as well. Who needs a little bit of room from you today?

Accepting Gifts

Luke 7:36–50

We have no idea why the woman in this story was labelled a sinner, though tradition has tended to accuse her of adultery or loose morals. Remember, a sinner could be anyone with a birthmark, someone in any way complicit with Rome, someone who picked grain on the Sabbath, someone of mixed heritage. She may have even been audacious enough in her sin as to try and learn from a rabbi or study the Torah, unfeminine and unacceptable roles for women at the time of Jesus. Whatever the reason for her label, she adds to it: she touches Jesus, possibly passing on her sin to him; comes in as an uninvited guest, affecting not only the dinner guests, but the house itself; and does something odd with ointment. In Matthew, Mark, and John, there is a parallel version of this story that both identifies the ointment as nard and declares the value of the ointment used—a year's wages, comparatively $100,000 in today's world. In the Hebrew Bible, prophets anointed kings with oil. The woman's act literally makes Jesus the *Christ*, Greek for "the anointed one."

Luke does not involve Judas, nor does he build up the extravagance of the gift (though the fact that it is in an alabaster jar speaks to its high value). Instead, Luke highlights the offense of Simon; the offering of the woman's presence, ointment, and tears shows hospitality greater than the host's.

Simon is worried about (no surprise) cooties, his reputation, and pro-priety. If Jesus really knows and speaks for God, how can he let a sinner touch him and risk defilement? He should rebuke her as unworthy or ask her to do the necessary penance before coming to him. Curiously, the Book of Common Prayer allows a priest to withhold communion from a parishioner who is unrepentant of notorious sins. In the past, this has been an effective stick to motivate people to be reconciled.

Jesus offers a different perspective: people in a state of notorious sin might just need the grace of God more than the healthy ones. Three years ago, a man I knew to have schizophrenia stood up and offered his own thoughts in the middle of my sermon. People looked for the doors. People might have looked for the police. I was scared, but I stayed still. He said what he wanted to and walked out. Maybe this was one of the few times in his life when people did not run away from him or silence him and he was able to leave church on his own terms. I don't know what it would be like to have this experience every week, but I wonder if it doesn't invite us to think about propriety in general. Manners are social conventions that help people know what to do, regulate behavior, and allow people to feel safe. When manners are used to dismiss, ridicule, or condemn, well, they are bad manners! I would pose the same for worthiness in worship and offer that what makes God's holiness so holy is that it cannot be compromised by "low" things.

Jesus is not trying to shame Simon, but to challenge our stereotypes of hospitality. Can we make room for someone to upset the applecart of our cultural expectations? Can we extend hope instead of our suspicions? I've heard that the surest sign of maturity is the ability to receive a compliment. Does our giving get out of whack because our ability to receive is compro-mised? As a host, I have a hard time receiving because I am so fixated on controlling the experience of my guests.

The woman's faith saves her. Luke is inviting salvation here and now. She, in spite of her reputation, offers a gift that is accepted. When we allow people who are often recipients of our charity or our derision to give to us, they enter into mutuality with us. Maybe Jesus is the first person to accept her care in a long list of tries, and in so doing she is validated as someone who is worthwhile. He forgives her sins by accepting her "tainted" touch. Maybe she is also saved from being spurned and isolated. And maybe, just maybe, we might accept a gift that restores someone.

Sowing Seeds

Luke 8:1–15

Luke is unique in naming the funding for Jesus's mission and ministry: women. Remember, Jewish women were culturally ordained as second-class citizens at the time of Jesus, unable to inherit property or own businesses outright. Without these "second-class" citizens, Jesus would not have had the ability to do what he did. Undoubtedly, Luke is putting women on the plain and inviting us to join him! Undoubtedly, Christianity began with females in leadership—women are named apostles, elders, and deacons—but over time began to adopt the dominant culture's preference of elevating men. Luke is asking his readers to resist this urge, to be countercultural, to remain on the plain.

This parable seems to be an easy one. Jesus tells the disciples what it means right after he tells it. Despite a fairly straightforward agricultural analogy, hard questions follow. What kind of soil are you? Are people one type of soil during a lifetime or several types all at once? Can you prove your soil's goodness with your produce? Do the fruits of faith feed the birds or someone else?

If you have a hunch as to your soil "type," how can you go from being thorny ground to good soil? How does rocky ground become fertile? What rocks would need to be crushed within yourself so that God's seed can take deeper root? What paths have you traveled so frequently that they are both harder and more condensed than rocks? How might you soften them? What is choking your joy, your ability to receive grace? It seems like each soil needs different rehabilitation. The sower should do some good shaming of that darn rocky soil. I am still trying to break the rocks of doubt from the soil of my life and deepen and irrigate the soil for God's Word, also expecting other people to do that themselves—and fast. Can we trust the growth and the fruit to God?

Why does the sower throw seeds where they cannot thrive? Could it be that God has such an abundance of resources that seeds can be wasted? Could it be that God has such profound patience that seeds that bear no apparent fruit can, by basic cultivation, churn the soil, break rocks, and weaken the root systems of weeds? Could God anticipate the birds in the story, like real birds, will excrete the seeds so they can grow and bear fruit somewhere else? Could we be patient, willing to take risks with God's abundant grace in our lives, willing to see where even the birds take the Word?

What is the "Word of God" being sown? Who sows the seed and gives the Word: God? Jesus? Us? I wish I were good soil, but thirty, sixty, or one hundred times more? That makes me feel really small, unimportant, anxious about my performance. But the sower doesn't invest more seed in the good soil or reward it with bejeweled scarecrows. The good soil's reward? Producing food for the hungry. Are we willing to feed a hungry world, whether they deserve it or appreciate it or not, with abundant grace and patience?

Jesus seems to tell parables (this is the first one of many to follow) in order to *confuse* people ("looking they may perceive and listening they may not understand"). Could it be if a parable seems to be really simple that an alarm should be sounding to indicate that we misunderstand? Seminary professor Steve Kraftchick compared parables to jokes: if you don't get a joke, explaining it will not likely result in laughter. He argued that parables are more the stuff of metaphor and irony than analogy. Jokes require us to understand language, like double entendres, puns, and alternate definitions that are hard to crack cross-culturally. Jokes require that we know the context. Metaphors about sowing seeds might only work for farmers, while we might not get past the literal sense. Is feeding the birds bad or is that the point? Do we wither when we hear the hundredfold because we feel unworthy? Could we make "bad" investments in folks of time and talent and care because God enjoys that as well? I'd certainly need a new wineskin to adopt these practices, let alone smile when I do them!

We return to the women. Jesus sows grace into them, serves as their rabbi, heals, touches, and includes them. And they bear fruit more than a hundredfold for Jesus's ministry through stories we continue to be inspired by today—out of "unfit" soil!

Order in the Chaos

Luke 8:22–25

In Genesis 1:1, God starts with a mess—with chaos. We don't know why God made this choice, but the rabbis reasoned that God's nature is to pull order out of chaos, to create real and meaningful communities out of primitive scrawls on the wall. In the Psalms, God creates sea monsters, Behemoth and Leviathan, just for the sport of it. Only God can corral these forces that eat humans for breakfast. So, if Jesus calms the winds of chaos, it is confirmation that he is God. It is an invitation for followers of Jesus to be God-like in helping reorder the chaos of our relationships and world.

Even a cursory read of this story suggests that Jesus was not worried about the chaos that so terrified the disciples—he was asleep in a boat that was simulating every ride at Six Flags at the same time and did not wake up until they roused him with their fear. Water was pouring into the boat and it still did not wake him up! Jesus either had a really clear conscience or was simply not afraid of the storm because he had already concluded that it was not detrimental to his health or safety, nor the well-being of his friends.

God is not afraid of apparent chaos like we are. Maybe the difference is that God knows where this is all going. If we only knew that we could ensure outcome X for our kids, partner, or parents by doing Y every day. If we knew that marriage counseling or dance lessons or even electro-shock therapy would make us more joyful people, most of us could make that happen. We struggle with uncertainty and often don't know or don't trust that we can weather the storms we encounter. We may not have the power to calm the winds and waves of chaos, but we can be a nonanxious presence through life's squalls.

This story asks us to consider our faith in the final outcome. Why do we waste so much energy and allow fear to dominate so many of our interactions? If God is always with us, then maybe it doesn't all depend on whether we hoist the sails now or scrub the mizzenmast. What if we trust our knowledge of God's redeeming power enough to live the rest of the story? Instead of treading water with all our might, perhaps we can float, confident that God will hold us up. This is an invitation to find calm within the storms instead of waiting until they end. Rather than tell people they should not be worried, we can be with them and bear witness that God is with them. Maybe it's enough to be present with and for each other.

26

When Pigs Fly

Luke 8:26–39

There are several oddities built into this story of the healing of the man from Gerasenes. Did he have multiple personality disorder, schizophrenia, or some other mental health disorder? He certainly was only barely alive, living, both literally and figuratively, among the tombs, unrestrainable, and naked—antisocial behavior attributed to demons.

Why drown innocent swine? Symbolically, swine are unclean animals to the Jews (because they are omnivores; only ruminants are kosher meats), but that does not seem a drownable offense. Taking the name Legion (a troop of at least 2,000 soldiers), the demon is a clear reference to Rome's might. Luke is clearly making a commentary on the fundamental uncleanliness and unholiness of the Roman Empire here with a prediction that the very strength of the empire, its military, will be drowned in chaos.

The greatest oddity of all, however, might be the crowd's reaction to seeing the transformation of the man they feared, undoubtedly avoided, and likely told stories about. They beg Jesus to leave. Rather than rejoicing that their distressed and diseased neighbor was brought back to health and sanity, they were afraid. It is almost as if they had become accustomed to the "monster" in their midst. Did they need to cast their fears upon him? Were they so incapable of imagining him as anything other than sick that his adoption of clothes and return to health was unbelievable and even undesirable? The poor man wants a fresh start, to go somewhere new with Jesus where he can be known as himself instead of the crazy, naked guy who lived like he was dead. No luck. Jesus sends him home to do the tough work of living into reconciliation.

Sometimes when I read scripture, I wonder what is wrong with the people in the story. How could anyone be afraid of healing and reconciliation? Then I remember how the stigmas of being incarcerated, diagnosed with a mental illness, issued a DUI, having gang-related tattoos live on. All of a sudden, a bizarre story about swine and hard-hearted people confronts my established prejudices and paper-thin faith in reconciliation and God's ability to accomplish genuine repentance.

At the same time, I am reminded of the value and difficulty of living out repentance with the people I have offended. It would be nice to drop a note in the mail and move on (I'd be pretty nomadic, though), but reconciliation is slow and complicated. Part of me wants to say that it always takes longer for the victim than for the perpetrator, but I am no longer convinced. Sometimes, the offender is unable to trust they will be seen as trustworthy. Reconciliation is to be lived out in the communities where things went wrong in the first place. Maybe this is why everyone is so afraid. Maybe this is why we pay more attention to pigs flying than to reconciliation. Why is it that the toughest and most needed reconciliations might only happen when pigs fly?

Jesus seems to be asking me who I have consigned to live among the tombs, when I will let them live again, how deeply I am able to trust forgiveness and reconciliation, and what I am most afraid of—the existence of disturbing people in my community or being reconciled with them.

27

The Importance of Touch

Luke 8:40–48

Jesus, unlike me, models distractibility for the sake of larger life at its best. He is on a mission to do something for someone important—a generous donor, a pillar of the community—when someone also in need comes his way. Undoubtedly, Jairus was annoyed. Every second counted as his daughter's life hung in the balance. And a cootified woman grabs Jesus's attention.

The woman in this reading epitomizes ritual uncleanliness. She has been bleeding for twelve years, and should be quarantined outside of communal contact. Her illness has taken all of her money and given her no relief. She, the townspeople, and her doctors all believed that her condition was earned. Her lack of healing was a lack of repentance or worthiness or both. Her exhaustion of financial resources was just another sign of her rejection by God. For her to knowingly touch someone else in such a state of impurity would compromise their purity as well; anyone she touched would be unclean. They would be required to perform ritual ablutions, avoid entrance into holy places, and avoid contact with others, lest the contagion of impurity be passed on yet again. Her touch would disqualify Jesus from entering Jairus's house. Life is perilous; by a single touch she could be beaten or stoned for contaminating someone else. Touch is dangerous. This is a woman who has only been touched by doctors, if at all, for twelve years. Their touches did not make her better or validate her humanity. This is a woman who is so desperate for human contact, for a touch that might give her some form of life, that life itself is an acceptable risk for her.

Touching even the clothes of someone else in Jewish tradition was forbidden. Some Jews wear a prayer shawl under their clothes as a reminder of their obligations to God. The shawl is called a *tallit* and has at least four fringes, called *tzitzit*, wound into braids and tied into knots for a total of 613, the number of commands or mitzvahs that the Pharisees extrapolated from the Torah (365 "dos"—one each day of the year—and 248 "don'ts"—one for each bone in your body, according to tradition). The tassels of the *tallit* are external signs of devotion to God and Torah, devotion that included avoiding the ritually unclean.

The woman touches Jesus on the *tzitzit*, a fringe tassel. The woman who has been living on the fringes touches Jesus on the fringes. The woman who has been denied touch by her culture, people, and religion touches Jesus in the most iconic personal element of that self-same legal code for purity. Somehow, her desperate faith makes her well, and Jesus knows it too. He beckons a crowd the size of fans leaving an NFL stadium to stop and say who touched him. The disciples are not amused. No doubt the woman is terrified, but she trusts that the agent of her healing will not abandon her if she is honest about her contact with the Torah through the *tzitzit*. She admits not only the touch, but the whole truth—she touched him in her uncleanliness and was healed. Jesus confirms what has already happened—she is healed and clean. Her terrible act in public results in the community hearing the news that she has been transformed and healed. This is definitely a gospel story—good news for someone who hadn't had any for a long time.

Who around us is untouchable and looking for recognition? Last year, I met with a family who was wrestling with depression, resources, and what to do next. They had no one to listen empathetically; they were desperate for a touch of support. They came into my office and said, "We are not parishioners and are not sure if we can even be here." I am often in a rush, but am glad that this time they heard back, "I'm so glad you are."

Offering blessings to people who are not sure they have earned them and striving to say "yes" on God's behalf is a privilege for a priest. But this story asks all of us to examine whether we see or are blind to untouchables in our world.

On Maundy Thursday a few years ago, I was cutting the hair of chronically homeless men and women after the bishop had washed their feet and they had been served lunch. I have no professional training, but do have two barber capes, two pairs of clippers (one for the shearing of sheep that I'd never used), and the little disposable neck wraps that go under the capes. I was there with one other volunteer who was a professional stylist. He struggled all day because of how dirty the people's hair was. He was right. Some had hair so greasy the clippers couldn't cut it, but the sheep shears worked! This might have been the one day of the year that these people could be touched with dignity and receive the undivided attention of someone to care for them. They were looking for a touch of love and no amount of grease or stigma could get in the way.

Luke invites us to live more deeply into relationship with those on the margins because of faith, not in spite of it. Their touch doesn't makes us unclean; rather, our touch reverses uncleanliness itself.

28

Touch and Nourishment

Luke 8:49–56

The story of the hemorrhaging woman who was healed by touching the *tzitzit* of Jesus comes immediately before this reading. Perhaps it is meant to inform this story as well.

Jesus has been asked by the synagogue leader to heal his daughter, who is at the point of death. We do not know if Jairus came to Jesus in faith or in desperation. Likely, he had heard of Jesus driving out unclean spirits and potentially other healing miracles.

Whatever social and religious power he holds in his community, Jairus has no power to help his daughter now, who is critically in need. Jesus does not comment on Jairus's depth of faith, but rather meets a man at his point of desperation. On the way, Jesus gets distracted by another need, the woman hemorrhaging. Undoubtedly, this proved irksome to Jairus, who must have heard with his own ears that an unclean woman had touched Jesus and potentially sullied his own cleanliness. Jairus doesn't insist on Jesus performing ritual oblations or waiting the Torah-prescribed twenty-four hours before coming to this village. Jairus is willing to bear ritual defilement in hope that his daughter can live. Desperation or faith? Sometimes, the line is thin. In today's world of efficiency, thanks to technology and Type A personalities, many of us have schedules that are full with good stuff, but with few, if any, margins that allow space for others. For ourselves. For life. It is never too late to make some room.

Unlike the woman in the previous story, Jairus was respected by the community (led the synagogue) and had resources (mourners were hired), but his need was similar to the ill woman: a touch that could bring life. When Jesus arrives, he is mocked for stating that the girl is not dead. Jesus is mocked for saying that a dead girl can be awakened to new life, but what if the doctors, family, and friends in attendance declared her dead before she was? What if, for fear of defiling themselves by touching a dead body, they never bothered to take her pulse? What if, seeing her in the throes of a serious illness, they played the percentages in their head and consigned her to death before she actually died? What if Jesus is willing to risk his own religious defilement to touch someone his culture claims cannot live again?

I made a friend in my Parables of Jesus class during seminary. We worked out and ate meals together while sharing stories of our upbringings and hopes for the future we shared. One day, on the way home from an event, he looked at me and said, "I have really enjoyed getting to know you, but before I can continue to trust you, I need you to know that I am gay." I was twenty-one and had grown up Southern Baptist. I had never met an openly gay person before and was really uncomfortable. I assured him that this would not threaten our friendship (but also assured him anxiously I was not gay). I sought advice from family and friends and heard: he is trying to corrupt you and if you invest in this friendship, you are condoning his sin. Instead, I stayed in relationship, and gratefully gained a lively and insightful friend—a person dead to so many others.

Even if the girl *was* dead and Jesus resuscitated her, the outcome is not significantly different: Jesus gives new life to someone who had none. He proves she is not a ghost and needs to be restored to her community by giving her food. Breaking and sharing bread were, then as now, signs of community and equality. I have never resuscitated someone from the dead, nor have I been directly involved in a faith healing through touch, but I have seen dead relationships resurrected by the bold efforts of people who risked defilement and damaged reputation, annoyance, and stress in order to reconcile and rehabilitate another. How do I provide to people who need the life support of dignified touch and the all-important but ordinary investment of a shared meal?

It is never too late to live into yourself; it just gets harder as we face not only change, but the inertia of habitual resistance to it as well. Jesus seems to model this advice in this reading and the previous one. The thing is, it doesn't seem to get harder for Jesus, it just seems to get harder for us. Maybe it is the community pressure that so often feels like snowballing or the inertia of inaction. May God give us the energy we need to push past our fear of uncleanliness and apparent death, to push past efficiency against distractions and our piety above others, and embrace living on the plain! It is not too late to love bigger. Every time we open ourselves to grace, as in prayer, the Holy Eucharist, and acts of loving-kindness, we are nourished for our journey toward larger life.

29

Bread for the World

Luke 9:10–17

The disciples need some empathy. "Good work, Jesus. Great way to take care of some more unclean spirits. But these folks are looking hungry and, well, we are feeling it ourselves. Send them away so they can get some nourishment (and we can too)." Unlike this story in Matthew, in which Andrew finds a young volunteer to share the loaves and the fishes, the disciples are the ones with the food; food that would give each of them a fair meal, but less than a taste for each in the crowd. It has been suggested that 90 percent of the Judean diet was bread—a two-pound loaf per person per day.[8] It took women five to six hours to do the daily grind, knead the dough, allow it to rise, and then bake the loaves. Scholars seem to disagree about how large each loaf was, but if we are generous, the disciples have the daily caloric and nutritional intake for five adults. The other 10 percent of the daily diet was usually wine, worse than three-buck-chuck by our standards, of extremely variable quality, as water was not always potable. Perhaps some olive oil or, if in luck, pomegranates or figs could supplement a meal. The disciples, living near Tiberius on the Sea of Galilee, had a nutritional edge over

---

8. Carol Meyers, *Rediscovering Eve: Ancient Israelite Women in Context* (Oxford: Oxford University Press: 2012), 130.

many, likely enjoying a regular addition of fish alongside bread. Still, they hardly had enough for themselves, and Jesus asked them to share?

The crowd of five thousand men (who knows how many woman and children alongside them) sit in groups. Some folks think that perhaps these groups offer food and take care of themselves. Others go for the strictly miraculous interpretation. Either way, Luke is very clear that what seems a scant amount to us can, when blessed by Jesus, result in sustenance beyond what we could ask or imagine.

Jesus does not ask us to actually share our lunch with others; food we have bitten off is not really proper fare to offer someone who appears hungry. However, he might ask us to share our lunch with someone by eating with them, by giving up the extra work time we could have squeezed in by chewing as we type. Instead of viewing our lunch break as precious alone time, might we make our empathy and companionship available to someone else? What is often alone time for us can be lonely time for someone else. If there is no one else around, we might give up being productive in exchange for breathing deeply, focusing on the meal before us: its flavors, its sourcing, and the hands that prepared it. These seem like scant offerings, but in the hands of Jesus they can go a long, long way.

At the Eucharist, we ask God to nourish not only our bodies with bread and wine, but also our spirits, to give us energy to be greater than ourselves. We don't eat much; a small wafer and a small sip, at most. We do not offer the finest fare; few people eat bread that tastes worse than a wafer or imbibe wine inferior to the chalice. I have never seen someone ask for more wafers to have more energy. We have come to believe, through practice, that a little goes a long way with God.

Sometimes, when I administer the bread at communion, I come close to running out: four wafers left and ten folks at the rail. There is often something left in reserve, but I usually begin splitting wafers so as not to disrupt the flow of the service. In half is fine, so is a quarter. As I offer the meager morsel I say, "The Body of Christ, the bread of heaven. God can do a lot with a little."

There are hundreds of people in deserted places and Jesus does not want us to send them away hungry. He bids us to offer the often drab and scant snacks we hoard as nourishment for a hungry world with the promise that God can do a lot with our little. What act of kindness, patience, or charity might you consider trusting to the hands of Jesus by sharing with another today?

30

Take Up Your Cross

Luke 9:21–27

Traditional depictions of the cross have been influenced by art and culture, its horror not always represented accurately. It seems the Persians imagined and initiated crucifixion; the Romans fine-tuned it. Crosses were used as ancient billboards to advertise the fate that awaited treason: slow, inhuman, public, humiliating death. Thieves had their hands or thumbs removed. (Jesus is crucified between two "bandits," better rendered "insurrectionists.") Wealthy turncoats were beheaded. Crosses were for the poor.

One way to die on a cross was by shock, which took only a few hours; another was asphyxiation, which could take days. In order to take in a breath, the crucified had to pull their body weight off of their lungs. Over the hours and days, fatigue would set in until the crucified suffocated. To prevent shock, Romans offered a mild sedative: wine mixed with myrrh (Jesus declined this).

Crosses were shaped like capital Ts, not lowercase ones. The upright section, similar to a railroad tie or telephone pole, was permanently installed in the ground just outside the city gate; the horizontal two-by-four fitted into a slot atop the T. Carrying the cross was not a heavy job, but it had a heavy outcome. Most people in the ancient world lived outside of a city's gates, but had to come inside to buy and sell. On their way in or out, they passed the advertisement for Roman authority and treason's consequence. Nails could not hold body weight, but were sometimes used for added cruelty. Ropes secured the condemned. Victims were crucified naked, shameful for the Jewish faith. Victims were crucified inches above the ground; arms and legs would be twisted to accommodate any height. Crucifixion required no ladders and could be done with two soldiers. The crucified could be mocked or spat upon at eye level. Sometimes wild animals ate the crucified. Some records indicate that crucified folks were stolen away in the night. The gladiators and slaves that revolted against Rome in the first century BCE, Spartacus among them, were crucified along the Roman highway in one-mile increments and left for years.

I do not believe Jesus is asking his disciples to endure a bunch of pain in order to follow him; he is not asking us to become masochists to prove our love to God or earn heavenly comforts at the expense of our bodies. Instead, Jesus could be asking us to risk treason against the powers of this world that dominate, isolate, and impair the children of God from living joyfully on the plain. I don't think Jesus is advocating anarchy, but asks us to challenge powers that degrade. We are not asked to take up guerilla tactics in resistance to the politics of our elected officials, but to challenge with integrity the politics that dominate. Crosses are not just political; some treason might be against prejudice at a club, bullying at work or in school. Jesus is asking us to step out on behalf of someone else. Too often, we hear the cross as a call to suffer instead of an invitation to share life with others. If we are hurting and no one is receiving life, surely Jesus wants us to get off such a self-imposed cross. If we are changing diapers, supplying food to the hungry, or taking time to listen to that annoying colleague so that life might increase, maybe it is worth staying where we are. If we are not uncomfortable on behalf of someone else, maybe it's an invitation to commit the treason of being vulnerable, of thinking about someone else a little harder, of giving someone a second chance. Unlike so many other commodities, the more love and empathy we give, the more we have to give. Some crosses are undoubtedly heavier and more legendary than others, but might we pick up even a teeny one today on behalf of someone else and thereby start to follow Jesus?

31

Transformation

Luke 9:28–43

Transfiguration is defined as a complete change of appearance.
The traditional approach to this reading is to understand it as a
vision of God's glory that is meant to sustain the disciples as well as modern
believers through periods of doubt or repentance. It is why this reading
always appears in our lectionary as a foretaste of Easter in Lent. The problem with this view is that the disciples don't really seem any wiser as Luke
progresses and are, just a few verses later, unable to drive out an unclean
spirit in Jesus's name. Spoiler alert: we need Lent every year because the
vision of coming glory at the transfiguration is not enough for us either.

Figuratively, the scene is spectacular. Three disciples get to see the
glory of God emanating from the face of Jesus, a testament to Jesus standing in God's presence just as Moses did atop Sinai when he received the
Torah. Jesus is clad in dazzling white, indicative of priestly garments.
Moses and Elijah show up. Elijah represents charismatic and prophetic
leadership; Moses the deliverer and lawgiver. Jesus stands easily in their
company and represents the fulfilment of both, with a little priestly ritual
cleanliness sprinkled on top. What we often miss is that the three of them
are talking. I wish I knew what the conversation was about. Did Jesus ask
Moses, "Remember when you talked about not working on the Sabbath
day? How about healing folks or rescuing donkeys out of wells? Those

seem like holy things to do, not just on any day, but all the more so on the Sabbath because it is supposed to be extraordinary." I wonder if Jesus told Elijah, "I remain inspired by how you confronted abuses of power by the king over ordinary folks like Naboth. Thanks for this example. But I take real issue with your killing the four hundred prophets of Baal. Seems like you chose to take revenge instead of giving an opportunity for repentance or offering compassion. I'm certain that two wrongs never make a right." I wonder what else Jesus said. I wonder how they answered. I wonder if they disagreed.

The disciples observed a conversation that was potentially critical. They were flabbergasted and wanted to consecrate it within a booth, a "tabernacle" like the one that once enshrouded the ark and served as worship headquarters throughout the Promised Land until the temple was built. They had likely heard conversations in synagogues between famous rabbis and the Torah, but had they ever had their own? The voice from heaven affirms, as it did at Jesus's baptism, that Jesus is beloved by God and worth listening to. It is unclear who the voice is talking to: the disciples, Moses, Elijah, or all three? Maybe Moses and Elijah needed to listen, even if only figuratively.

Might it be possible that the voice from heaven is also speaking to us? Might the voice be encouraging us as children of God to have our own conversations anchored in reason, tradition, and scripture?

Jesus disagreed with a strict application of the Sabbath. He chose to "work," knowing it was unbiblical to heal on that day. I disagree with the injunction against wearing garments made of only one kind of polymer; cotton polyester blends have made me much more presentable. I eat shellfish and sometimes pork. I don't cover my head and I often shave. I disagree frequently with the Torah. This may sound like a slippery slope, but our Christian culture told us a long time ago that we do not have to wear tasseled garments, kippahs, yarmulkes, or cover our heads in public.

Perhaps the conversation we are meant to have about and with scripture is not whether it's okay to break a rule, but whether a rule guides us into larger life. Do we obey the law and miss the point? Do our actions resonate with the resurrected Jesus? Does our conversation with scripture include others? Do we trust that our voice is worth listening to and developing? I wonder if we had more holy conversations with the Bible whether we would grow into larger life, as a community and as individuals. I wonder, since culture is increasingly fragmented when disagreements emerge, if churches shouldn't be precisely *the* places where adults can gather, respectfully offer their vulnerabilities and opinions, disagree, and then worship together as a community unified not in the finer points of doctrine but the larger life of mission.

This passage ends with a story that reveals the disciples have not learned who Jesus really is or who he asks them to be. They are full of the vision of glory, perhaps putting Jesus right back in to the messiah of their dreams category instead of accommodating the Messiah of God's imagination. There is a difference between hearing and listening. The first is the sense and ability to record information; the second is about making space for another person or for information, appreciating a position or a context, being willing to change one's mind, or expand our vision for even the most unlikely position. The disciples had a glimpse of glory and nothing changed. They heard the words, and nothing changed. We need not only to see a different figure, but to hear a different message, so that we can be transformed and offer transformation for the world.

32

Neighbors

Luke 10:25–37

In 722 BCE, the Assyrian Empire conquered the ten northern tribes of Israel and purposefully displaced them throughout their massive empire, creating a turnover of ethnicity, language, custom, and religion. The Samaritans worshipped atop Mt. Gerazim and considered themselves faithful Jews. Their southern neighbors, the tribes of Judah and a remnant of Levi, disagreed and found the Samaritans as bad as, if not worse than, Gentiles. Good Jews walked around Samaria and avoided talking with or touching Samaritans. "Good Samaritan" was an oxymoron; no such thing existed. Good Benedict Arnold. Good Robert Mugabe. Good Adolf Eichmann. You get the point.

Which was a neighbor? The truth is, all of the people in the story are neighbors. All of the people in the story act like neighbors. Only one acts like the neighbor you would like when you are in need. Maybe. Jesus invites us to take a leap of action instead of leap of faith, to have compassion on those in need regardless of their religion, race, political party, or even if they have hurt us in the past. I think we get this, even though we struggle to live it. At the same time, I wonder if, like me, there are people in your life that you think so poorly of that you would almost rather die than receive help from? I think I might prefer death to Osama bin Laden's help, or to the help of a few other people from my past. If they helped me,

I would have to see them as human, I would maybe owe them some debt of gratitude or reciprocity. If they helped me, I would no longer be able to wholly dismiss them or feel morally superior to them. If they helped me, I would no longer be in control of the relationship; we would both have agency, we would be equals of sorts. The man in the story is too hurt to resist being helped. He might prefer death to the uncleanliness that will happen from being touched. He might be looked at suspiciously by his community from here on out.

Maybe Jesus is asking us to consider whether we value principles, pettiness, and control over life or whether we might allow folks who owe us, are worse off than us, are looked down upon by us, or are unknown to us to come onto the plain with us. Reconciliation happens when we receive; sometimes giving is a way of keeping someone else at arm's length. Perhaps we do not need or want the gift, but our neighbor wants to connect to us by giving. Maybe Jesus is asking us what kind of neighborhood we yearn to live in—a mount or a plain?

33

Purpose and Joy

Luke 10:38–42

This story has been misused in a myriad of ways. Kitchen work is inferior to studying and learning. Without Martha's hosting, the studying and learning would not have been possible. Personality Type B is better than Type A and Martha should not be so worried about the meal.

Martha is a busybody. Martha is a dedicated and attentive host who cares for her guests. Real faith is about stillness, solitude, and contemplation, not bustling. "Pray as though everything depends upon God, but act as though everything depends upon you."[9]

Both girls have broken cultural norms. Martha has invited Jesus into her home. Party invitations, along with home ownership, were distinctively male privileges. Martha has exerted uncharacteristic agency and boldness and Jesus responded favorably. Her hospitality allows for teaching, warmth, and connection with Jesus himself. She is a model to be emulated in this way and Luke has reenacted the message of the "good" Samaritan through Martha: be a neighbor like this.

Mary has chosen to sit at Jesus's feet and listen. This was the normal posture for students of a rabbi. It was intimate, but also reserved along

---

9. Source debatable—Augustine, Ignatius, or unknown: https://www.catholic
.com/magazine/online-edition/st-ignatius-said-what.

with Torah study for men. Jesus not only condones Mary studying the Torah and acting as a disciple, but endorses her. Hopefully, we encourage and appreciate God's widespread invitation to learn at God's feet and be nourished at God's table; that all people may study, learn, and worship in full membership.

The rub. Martha expects Mary to emulate and practice Martha's faith and values. Martha is disappointed that Mary has chosen listening over creating the environment for others to listen. Martha is not asking Jesus to tell Mary to fit into the normal woman's role; Martha already stepped outside it by inviting Jesus herself. She is asking Jesus to tell Mary that her ministry is more important than Mary's, that serving on the altar guild is more important than worshipping in the pew, or that cooking in the soup kitchen is more important than walking the labyrinth. Martha's issue is not that serving and hosting count less than studying and learning, but that she has become distracted by other expressions of piety and being in the world to the point of asking Jesus for conformity.

We all know what it is like to be disappointed when others do not step up to help in important work, especially our brothers and sisters. Jesus offers the idea that in the closet of faith, thought and practice are just a few of many garments, some of which fit all of the time, some just seasonally, and some never feel right for us, though others enjoy them. We are not obligated to wear piety that doesn't fit us, but we're invited to come and see, wear and exchange, and enjoy. What if we exchange our anxiety and distraction for confidence in purpose and joy in service? Whichever type we engage in, let us pick the better part.

34

The Lord's Prayer

Luke 11:1–13

Luke offers a more compact version of the Lord's Prayer than we typically use. It was normal for a rabbi to teach followers how to pray; the disciples make that clear by asking Jesus to do for them what John did for his followers. I have to admit, I prefer "Our father" to Father, mainly because it reminds me that I am not an only child, but that God's family extends far and wide, that my siblings in the Lord include dysfunctional and difficult ones. I am pretty sure Luke implies this. Father, *Abba*, is not just a word of intimacy, but a position of stewardship and responsibility. The paterfamilias was the head of the Roman household, directly responsible for seeing to the dignity, advancement, and care of every member of the household, family, servants, and contractors alike. In my home, the paterfamilias was my mom and it is worth noting that many of us need to address God as "Parent" or even "Mother."

Surely, we do well to remember God as greater than Father, the One who cares for every member of the household, holds their joy and dreams, and advocates for them. And that is exactly how God's name is holy, extraordinary. Remember, our Jewish roots assign an actual name to God, THE Y-WORD, which sounds like a breath. God animates the human being, sculpted from clay in Genesis 2, by breathing God's own name into it. God's name is life: it is the first thing we say when we are born and the last to leave our lips when we die. Our *nefesh*, Hebrew for "soul," resides not in our chest, but in our trachea, the point of breath and the intonation of God's name. Breathing is ordinary. We take in oxygen and breathe out poison, carbon dioxide. God's name is hallowed by us not only because it is the breath of life that we so often take for granted, but how we choose to breathe out life for one another instead of poison. The words of our mouth and actions of our being are being called into scrutiny every time we pray as Jesus wills us to. May we breathe God in *and* out.

Your kingdom come. This kingdom functions as a kin-dom, not a hierarchical system. We so often pray this, but really mean "my ideas about God and others come." Maybe Jesus invites us to ponder God's perspective on us instead of getting so hung up on our perspectives on God. And should we do so, to join with God in establishing God's family on earth.

Our daily bread. A reminder: 90 percent of the average daily diet was a 2-pound loaf of bread that took upwards of 5½ hours of work to produce each day. Jesus teaches his disciples to focus on what they need for the day. I am a planner and take some pride in making sure that when one jar of jam, box of detergent, or roll of paper towels runs out, there is at least one ready in the pantry to replace it. I often think upon achieving any milestone, what's next? Constant planning and forecasting is the ultimate foil of addicts of any kind. The uncertainty of the future can be fun, but can also be crushing. Maybe Jesus is trying to get us to focus on being present now. A therapist once offered the 90/10 rule: intense emotions such as anger at kids, spouses, or coworkers is usually based on 10 percent of the present circumstance and 90 percent of the past. We are invited to pray in such a way as to stretch into our present, no matter how mundane or magnificent it may seem, to be here, alert now, with ourselves and our colleagues. There is value in Bil Keane's adage "Yesterday is history. Tomorrow is a mystery. Today is a gift. That's why they call it 'the present.' "[10] Would that we might receive each present moment, each breath of God's name, as a gift from God, especially in prayer.

---

10. Bil Keane, *The Family Circus*, 1994.

Forgive, for we forgive. This prayer assumes we do. Ugh. God, treat us as we treat others? I'd rather pray, "God, treat me much better than I treat others, forgive me when I don't, can't, won't forgive others." I am pretty sure that this is how God will work in the end, but Jesus is asking us to stretch ourselves before God *now*, to consider our common humanity. We are often fully aware of why we were curt to Aunt Martha at Thanksgiving (and it wasn't because we were possessed by pure evil as much as tired from travel and being asked for the hundredth time if we wanted more turkey). We are rarely aware of the context for actions by others that adversely affect us. Jesus asks us not just to forgive, but to cancel debts while still lending more. Jesus asks us to do these things, and to ask God's help in doing them.

Do not bring us to the time of trial. This could be asking God to spare us from temptation, but I wonder if it might also be about our predilection to put God in places where God doesn't fit. After 9/11, a few religious leaders claimed that God orchestrated the event as a punishment for gay rights and the NAACP. God doesn't bring us to these beliefs, but we go and worship ourselves in all our pettiness by slapping "God" on top of these atrocities. May we carefully discern God's lead from our own.

Teach us to pray. Perseverance in prayer begs us to reconsider laundry-listing God about our wants and likes and, instead, to repair damaged relationships, feed the hungry, appreciate the small things, and even the things that do not inherently please us. To do good things instead of asking God to do them. To live larger lives as a prayer. I am no mystic, but my most powerful prayer experiences have not usually involved talking, but simply being aware that God is present with me and trying to honor that presence with my interior dialogue, with awe, and with wonder. Praying shapes what we believe and how we interact and what we pursue. We will always have more to learn, but noticing the absolute closeness of God's presence, as close as our breath, is a good place to start.

There are times when my kids have asked for eggs or fish and I have responded with scorpions and stones (venom and burdens). Fortunately, there are more times when I resisted such responses for the sake of the relationship. Prayer might be about cultivating the kind of relationship with ourselves, with God, and with one another that does exactly this, slows our reptilian impulses just enough that we remember that we are irrefutably connected to one another and to God. We can do and be and pray larger.

35

Do Justly, Love Mercy

Luke 11:37–54

Jesus takes to task the most devoted church members of his day—members of religious orders, clergy, experts in canon law, and theologically informed Bible study leaders. Perhaps you are not one of these people. You can breathe a little easier. A little.

Pharisees were the first people you would go to for advice, care, help with your rent. And Jesus starts with them. He asks them to consider whether their hand-washing etiquette is more than just ritual. I ritually "wash" my hands each Sunday before the Eucharist with distilled water. There is no soap, nor friction, nor lather applied at the credence table. It is a symbol of a desire to have clean hands at the Lord's table. The tradition is not effective sanitation, it's only helpful in guiding our intentions. This same practice could be unhelpful if we viewed it as effective in itself or if we refused the Eucharist from "unwashed" hands. Jesus not only asks religious devotees to bring their reason to bear on their faith and practices, but all of us.

Traditions help the fiddler on the roof keep her balance, but can also keep her saddled to the roof in a lightning storm. Jesus invites the Pharisees, and us as well, to have a reasonable faith, to more explanation in our hearts than "because we have always done it this way."

Woe to the folks who pick and choose when to apply reason to tradition at the exclusion of others; they are like unmarked graves, full of death that not only threatens to defile, but to engulf others. I don't think Jesus is warning against tradition that is not logical or sensible; mystery is at the heart of faith. I think he is warning against tradition without reason to rank us above others instead of as an accountability measure. Tithing on is great, as long as we do not use the practice to privilege ourselves above others. Respecting the sanctity of sanctuaries with silence is great as long as it does not exclude families. Leviticus calls certain sexual acts abominations, but uses the same term for garments made of two different fabrics (cotton-polyester blends—God's gift to Southerners with mediocre ironing abilities—are not just unkosher, but abominable), shellfish (who doesn't love a good crawfish boil?), and wizardry of any kind (including horoscopes and fortune cookies, even if they are just for fun). Jesus asks us to be reasonable with our scrutiny of tradition. If we will say the last three practices are unreasonable and no longer apply, then why do we so often hang on to the first because "it has always been this way"?

Lawyers don't come out much better. Lawyers, says Jesus, are all too deft at using the finer points of the law to introduce the heavier loads of burden. Perhaps you did the right action, but did you have the right intention? You have been washing your hands for years before eating to protect your ritual purity, but did you use well water, river water, or rain water, or don't you even know that each of these has a varying efficacy? Did you offer folk any help in getting the "better" water for themselves to drink or wash with? At the end of the day, their acts of worship in discerning better from best result in shame and estrangement, not reconciliation or forgiveness. They build tombs to the prophets to lionize their importance, but neglected to internalize the words of the same prophets—God has shown us what the Lord requires: do justly, love mercy, walk in humility with God. Holding both standards and compassion is about as hard as holding onto God's immanence and transcendence at the same time. Jesus takes us to task when we give up this exercise.

As a kid I was told how awful adherents of other religions were; how shameful it was when they did not repent and become Christians the first time that they heard the "good news." The folks who espoused this position had grown up in Christian homes, communities, and churches; they never had to accept a religion at the expense of their family or identity. These people levied judgment without compassion. As a white, straight, Christian man, I can enjoy my privileged position and then be shocked others want equal protections under the law, or I can accept Jesus's invitation to begin with compassion instead of competition. It is the inside of the cup, our motives, rather than our outward behavior, which Jesus points toward.

36

Breathe Life

Luke 12:1–12

The irony of parents and grandparents trampling one another on Black Friday to offer Christmas joy is not, it seems, a recent novelty. The crowds looking to gain wisdom, healing, or a touch from Jesus trample one another. Sometimes I ask people what they most want for their church and their response is "growth." They usually mean the measurement in Sunday attendance and, while I think this would be great, I am also reminded that the fastest growing masses in the body are cancers and that numeric growth is not necessarily a sign of health. There could be thousands of people, trampling one another to get to Jesus. I once worked at a Christian school owned by a church of five thousand–plus members. A female teacher was fired for being pregnant and unmarried. They hired a young man as her replacement—the father of the child! Beware of the yeast of the Pharisees and trampling one another en route to Jesus.

Nothing will remain secret. A favorite fear tactic in the church of my youth was the idea that when we die, everything we have ever done will be played on a movie screen for the world to see. My grandmother would see all of my thoughts as well as my deeds. The shame and humiliation of this idea did not, oddly enough, whip me in to shape, but made me despise my own mind. I cannot imagine that this is what Jesus meant. Rather, to use an AA phrase, we might be "only as sick as our secrets." The shame we cover only breeds more shame, self-loathing, and fear. The weight of our hypocrisy easily exhausts all the energy we could have put into reform or just plain authenticity. What if we could hear one another's shame and fear in the light, so none of us had to live in the dark? I have known good parents who have struggled with their kids in silence, lest they be judged as poor examples or not strict enough. Why do we do this? Are we so threatened in our own identities that we cannot even hear the struggles of someone else? Beware of the yeast of the Pharisees.

Fear the one who can throw you into hell. *Gehenna* in Greek, *Ge-Hinnom* in Hebrew, "the valley of Hinnom." The Hinnom valley is just outside the city walls of old Jerusalem and is the closest low point, where the blood of sacrifices from the temple naturally flowed. Here the dregs of sacrifices were burned or ashes interred, along with any other trash from the city. It was also the place where Molech was worshipped; parents offered their firstborn sons, who represented a family's future, namesake, and most-prized possessions, as human sacrifices to appease the gods. Kings of Judah did this alongside pagans. Trash is not tortured, it is destroyed.

God does not ask for our firstborn; we thought that up ourselves. How many of us have spent our life afraid that God will punish us in hell forever while paradoxically saying that God is love and that God came to save the world? What if the hell we are to fear is the place where garbage is incinerated, not tortured, where the refuse of our pious offerings flow, where we burn up our future to appease false gods? We rarely need God's help to get there. I have been on many visits to these very real hells where the doors are well-marked with caution tape. But I still go.

God's eye is on the sparrow. God knows the numbers of hairs on our heads, which is not a warning, but a revelation of intimacy. How much more will God look out for us, how much more does God long for us to be free from our fears of God, and how much will God build bridges across the fears we have for one another. We do not need to fear missing out on Jesus or competing for God's favor to the point of trampling our neighbor or sanitizing our hypocrisy. We could throw all that into hell where God would love to burn the trash that separates us from one another and Life.

How do we acknowledge Jesus, the Son of Man, before others? Maybe by acknowledging Jesus in one another—enough to avoid trampling them or pushing anyone into a trash heap to appease the gods of our pettiness. Sometimes we do not know what to say. Take a deep breath and let the Holy Spirit inspire us. Growing at the expense of another is exactly what cancer does, what trampling represents. If we could breathe together and respect God's presence in the breathing, we might find ourselves living far from the hells of our creation and into the life God wills for us.

37

The Choices We Make

Luke 12:22–34

Worry is better translated "anxiety" in this reading. What's the difference? Worry seems to be more about giving into and dwelling upon troubles and dis-ease while anxiety might be better understood as energy with nowhere to go. Don't be anxious about your life and body and what you will eat or wear. Jesus may be speaking to those with means here; these would be terribly harsh words to starving, naked, and sick people without means.

The omnivore's dilemma is what to eat, given that there are so many choices. I spent a year living in Germany with the largest grocery store offering about six choices of breakfast cereal, four of them different kinds of muesli. Excessive options are overwhelming, even debilitating. My brain quickly goes to buyer's remorse. I should have picked the coconut muesli instead of the coconut cluster muesli. Am I missing out because of the lack of crunch? With too many variables to meaningfully compare (and with the outcome not significantly altered anyway), my brain revs up energy without a clear channel for it. Anxiety. Not necessarily a feeling at all, but more of a dumping ground for difficult-to-identify-energy. What to eat, not whether to eat. What to wear, not whether to wear. These are problems for people who have choices. Odd that our power to choose can be so disempowering.

Today is not about cereal either. Jesus asks, even as we have needs and wants, where is our treasure? That is where our heart will be. In the twenty-first century we tend to the think of our heart as the center of our being, of love and emotion, and even our soul. Ancient people identified the heart as the center of the will; today most of us would locate our will in our brain. Where your treasure is, there is your will. When our wills wrestle with what to eat and how to dress, assuming we have these choices, we are anxious and preoccupied. We end up absent, stressed, distracted, and overenergized. Jesus invites us to be preoccupied with the same things that God is preoccupied with: the family of God and that which does not wear out.

I like to cook and enjoy hosting friends. More than cooking, I like to succeed. I like for people to enjoy what I make. I can spend an entire evening trying to evaluate, based on both verbal and nonverbal cues (and possibly an algorithm I am still piloting), not only whether I succeeded, but give myself a grade to match. (I believe in grace, so I usually offer myself a 2 percent margin of error.) Meals that were designed to connect have, more than once, done the opposite in my brain. I am prone to anxiety in these ways, so I go out of my way to make sure I treasure some of the same things God does.

Brené Brown offers a helpful practice in her "Daring Greatly" curriculum that takes me out of my anxious brain: permission slips.[11] An exercise in intention setting, a permission slip is usually on a sticky note or a scrap of paper. I write down the permission I need to be more fully present, to invest my anxious energy in the moment instead of the cuisine evaluation. I give myself permission to make an edible meal. I give myself permission to waste time at a conference. I give myself permission to leave my house as is instead of cleaning. Sometimes I even advertise my permission slip—please join us for dinner and it will be casual; I am not even cleaning the house. While this may be a little too revealing, perhaps there are other anxious folks out there. Food or clothes may not be your thing. Catching instead of fishing. Completing a marathon instead of enjoying running.

11. Brené Brown, *Dare to Lead* (New York: Random House, 2018), 53–54.

Many of us wrestle with unchanneled energy and treasure things that are actually not that valuable. Jesus is asking us to live into our values, to enjoy exercise instead of completing a marathon, to cultivate authentic relationships instead of being the host with the most.

Jesus says more about birds and flowers. God cares for them. Flowers are beautiful, as we are to God. God is pleased to give us abundance. We choose whether we enjoy it or not by our practices and our anxieties. A former teacher suggested that we often fail to find our treasure because we look in the wrong places. I commend a practice he suggested: over the next month, whenever your mind wanders, allow it to go, but write a brief note about where it went. At the end of the month, find your treasure by reading your journal. Note what preoccupies you. Heavenly treasures and currencies of grace and presence are too valuable to miss out on.

Parables of Faith

Luke 13:18–21

Mustard seeds start small and grow into large bushes. Faith does not come all at once, but goes through stages of growth. I sure hope my faith continues to grow far beyond what was planted. Similarly, yeast is microscopic, but makes all the difference in rising dough and making bread nourishing. I hope my faith not only grows, but nourishes others.

There are a few oddities in Jesus's analogies here. Mustard seeds are not the "smallest" of seeds. Birds are not really desirable in gardens, as they tend to eat the produce. Mustard is an invasive plant, much like mint. Its roots spread underground and uproot adjacent plants. Mustard, like mint, has a very distinctive flavor and its flavor can be contagious so that adjacent grains and fruits begin to taste "mustardy" by just being in their proximity. Large bushes often outgrow other plants in the garden and create huge swaths of shade, which can be detrimental to the growth of other plants.

Yeast is not bad; Jewish people eat it fifty-one weeks a year. But it didn't come from a packet. Leaven came from either the air or from sourdough. At the Passover, there was not enough time for the yeast to do its thing before the people were to escape Pharaoh's slavery in Egypt. Matzah, flat bread, was the result. During Passover each year, yeast is eschewed and the home is cleaned from all its residues, especially the pantry, refrigerator, and oven. Yeast came to be connected with the ordinary, unleavened bread with the extraordinary.

How is the kingdom of God like a weed whose roots and flavor are invasive and, when full grown, harbors enemies of other garden plants and blocks the sunlight necessary for their growth? Best I can imagine, the kingdom of God is not only in the obvious—strawberries or the beautiful produce at Whole Foods Market—but precisely in the mundane. God's presence is in mangers, beggars, televangelists. I imagine that God's desire is for our *entire* lives to taste like and be rooted in the kingdom of God so much so that our faith spreads to everything around us. The faith God wills for us cannot be contained, sown only in small patches in the gardens of our lives. It always seeks to overrun the entire pasture. Why would we purposefully deny nutrients to the other parts? Precisely so that they cease to grow and our lives can be all the more invaded by God. Why would we want to harbor our enemies, the birds, the ones who eat the sower's seed (Luke 8:4–15)? Perhaps because a hungry world needs nourishment and weeds are the only things that grow fast enough to keep up? Once again, perhaps God is not only in the pious or the pure, but in the ordinary, the yeast, the weeds, the places we think God cannot be.

Faith can seem oxymoronic. How we often settle for an easy faith, for loving things that are easy to love. Consider one of my favorite hymns:

All things bright and beautiful, All creatures great and small,
All things wise and wonderful, The Lord God made them all.
Each little flow'r that opens, Each little bird that sings,
He [God] made their glowing colors, He [God] made their
tiny wings.[12]

What if mustard seed faith is about loving things that are intrinsically difficult to love, as in the Monty Python version:

---

12. Richard Proulx, "All Things Bright and Beautiful," *The Hymnal 1982*, #20.

All things dull and ugly, All creatures short and squat,
All things rude and nasty, The Lord God made the lot.
Each little snake that poisons, Each little wasp that stings,
He made their brutish venom. He made their horrid wings.[13]

It is the ugly, broken parts of myself, my family, my faith, and the
world that God might be asking me to love on this journey through Luke
and to nourish with a little more grace in this life. The leaven of the kingdom of God might just be in the ordinary, in you and me—in everyday
holiness that feeds the world.

13. Lyrics by Eric Idle, "All Things Dull and Ugly," *Monty Python's Contractual
Obligation Album*, Charisma Records, 1980.

39

Party Invitations

Luke 14:8–24

Sometimes called the parable of the wedding banquet, this might be better considered "the parable of the megaparty." Who knows what the dinner guest had in mind with the phrase about eating bread in the kingdom of God; most likely it refers to a restoration of the "golden age" under David and freedom from Roman hegemony and its tax burden. A real kingdom. Real bread. Jesus counters with a story about a party, snubbing, reciprocity, and an invitation to grace.

In the ancient world, as so often is the case today, accepting an invitation to a party was also accepting an obligation to one day return the favor. Parties were probably more about establishing and maintaining a social order and a network of alliances than about true celebration with a community. It was dangerous to accept an invitation that could not be directly reciprocated. It meant that one day the godfather might ask you to do a favor, a favor that you could not refuse. . . . So many who are invited either don't want to be obligated or are rejecting peership with the host. And they make some transparently lame excuses. Who buys land without seeing it first? This may have been a real practice in antiquity and perhaps there are venture capitalists who buy parcels sight unseen because either their intelligence is so good or the price is so low. However, having taken possession of the land, the owner could easily wait a day to survey it. Same with the oxen. I have only known one person who bought a car without haggling at the dealership, but even he took it for a test drive. Who buys oxen without trying them or checking their teeth?

So the party thrower has been rejected by the guests of honor. But this party must go on. All sorts of undesirables are not invited, but are then compelled and forced to come. The intended guests miss the party completely. This parable has been explained in the following ways, which I believe to be wrong, both contextually and theologically:

- A thinly veiled allegory for the Jewish rejection of Jesus and the ascent of Christians as God's chosen people. Beyond the flagrant anti-Semitism here, which seems unlikely considering Jesus was Jewish himself, there is really no response required from the hearer with such an interpretation.

- A dangerous invitation about partying in heaven or burning in hell. The parable itself has no mention of eternity.

- A scheme to obligate all of the working poor to the party thrower so that he can one day revenge himself against the party poopers. The invitation of the poor and lame and crippled, and their subsequent compulsion, seems the opposite of obligation—these are people who cannot pay back a favor of any magnitude. This is the opposite of an obligation and therefore, a true celebration.

Jesus's riposte to the blessing of eating bread in the family of God is to describe what sorts of people choose to eat God's bread. Rarely are the culturally elite favored. Instead, it is the lame, the crippled, the blind. Sinners. People who have so little that they cannot be worried about obligation because they are concerned with survival. Grace is a gift and not an obligation. God's party is so bold that it will go on, with or without the presence, enjoyment, or approval of those initially invited—including me when I put myself in this story. My feelings of unworthiness or judgment are just as lame as the excuses of the originally invited guests. God hopes you and I will not wait. I am sure God hopes we will make sure that everyone we run into, known or unknown, liked or disliked, deserving or undeserving, knows they are invited too.

40

Taste and Welcome

Luke 14:25–35

A word about salt. Morton® has made salt both common and cheap. White, granular, and uniform, it is used for taste more than any other substance and gets more than a little blame for hardening arteries. In the ancient world, salt was limited, expensive (it's the root of the word *salary*), and necessary. Without refrigeration, meat could be salted, smoked, consumed, or else must be tossed out or burned up. Without salt, health was threatened instead of the current fear of eating too much of it. In biblical times, salt was mined or taken from the sea in salt pans to evaporate; salt crystals were rarely, if ever, white or uniform in size, color, or taste. Salt came in a variety of colors and flavors, each determined by the trace minerals from the deposit. Pink Himalayan salt is a novelty now; mined salt was the rule then.

In Matthew 5:13, Jesus says, "You are the salt of the earth." I wonder if Jesus was talking about the uniqueness of salt. The salt of the earth varies in flavor and texture and color, just as real communities of diverse people do. How can we lose our saltiness? Maybe by picking uniformity instead of unity as the goal of discipleship. Maybe we are the salt of the earth exactly when we celebrate and trust in our unique history, experience, and theology. Maybe we lose our saltiness when we make doctrine the criterion for admission to the Lord's table instead of grace and with agreement as the basis for membership instead of commitment. The miracle of Jesus was that he got Simon the Zealot and Matthew the tax collector to eat together for three years even though they categorically hated each other. That's pretty salty. Flavor like that sure would enrich the taste of the world and preserve life that could nourish a whole bunch of people. Maybe we are asked to disagree and respect one another openly. Maybe we are asked to listen to the dissenting viewpoint of our neighbor appreciatively, grateful for how it informs their faith, without having to be converted. Maybe we are asked to not just tolerate diversity, but celebrate it.

I am a mathematician by training, not a chemist. But I do understand that salt can really only lose its saltiness when the sodium molecule is completely severed from the chloride. Dissolving salt molecules in water does not produce this end, only splitting the molecule removes saltiness. Can it be that Jesus wills us to hold separate elements together, to bring them to the Lord's table in unity, and warns us against the only way faith loses its ability to accentuate flavor and sustain nourishment—schism? Maybe Jesus asks us to go back and pick up the pieces, not of former doctrines or earlier opinions, but of the relationships that were tied to them. I am often called to re-member, to reattach to the body of Christ even if only in my imagination, with those from whom I am separated: my youth pastors and Christian school teacher peers for their intentions and limitations instead of their failings. I am asked to see them as bearers of God's grace as well. I don't have any trade secrets for staying unified amid diversity, but commitment and compassion are necessary. Sounds like a flavor our world could really use and enjoy this time through Luke, and a cost worth counting and paying.

41

Abundant Love

Luke 15:1–32

This reading is long, but it is critical to have the three parts of what seem like different parables; otherwise, we focus on prodigal sons instead of lost sons. The sheep and coins are not prodigal.

Domesticated animals differ from their wild counterparts in DNA; they have been bred for traits desirable to humans: a wild chicken lays an egg a month, as opposed to the domesticated chicken's egg per day. Also, they are dependent upon humans. Domesticated sheep need a shepherd to move them from overloading the carrying capacity of the land, lest they eat not only the blades of grass but also the root and so destroy their future. They need shepherds for protection because they do not live in craggy habitats that allow for ready escape, but in pens and on hillsides, and because their horns have been purposefully bred smaller. Domesticated sheep have been taught and altered by humans to rely on shepherds to care for them. If a domesticated sheep wanders, it is not because it is stupid, but because it trusts the shepherd.

No shepherd leaves ninety-nine sheep to pursue one. No shepherd leaves ninety to pursue ten. A solo shepherd cuts their losses, lest a wolf come and decimate the flock. In the story, Jesus tells about a bad shepherd, one who is so loss averse that he abandons the other ninety-nine. If we push too hard on this, we might find ourselves identifying with the ninety-nine and feeling, well, exposed by God's pursuit of the errant one. We might even find ourselves righteously indignant. God throws a party for the one who wanders, not for the ninety-nine who stay? Not quite. God throws a party because the flock is intact.

It is even more clear in the coin story because the women lost the coin herself—coins do not wander off. She cannot bear to be without her coin and throws a mighty celebration when she finds it because nothing was, indeed, lost.

The story about two sons is, therefore, not about prodigals, but about the lost being restored and the flock being intact. There are two threats to this. First, the younger son wants to be on his own. Perhaps his request for the inheritance is tantamount to wishing that his father was dead, but I doubt this, as I have parented a teenager. More likely, he, like so many of us, forgot the big picture when he saw an opportunity. We don't know how he loses everything; dissolute living can mean a panoply of things, including a downturn in the markets. We just know the older brother believes his brother has spent the money on prostitutes (which might be a simple suspicion or might reference a typical biblical usage of prostitution for religious infidelity, because pagan cults had sacred prostitutes). He comes to his senses when feeding swine and wishing for their food. The dad has been looking for the boy since the boy left and runs to greet him, hardly honoring social decorum. Dad interrupts the boy's penance speech and gives the younger son items that don't, in fact, belong to dad anymore. (He already divided the inheritance, which means he is literally giving the younger son possessions of the older.) In the biblical world, the eldest son received 66 to 90 percent of the inheritance, the second eldest son the residual, the remaining daughters and sons nothing. The son completes the flock by not only coming back, but by being received with full membership.

Second, the elder brother threatens the intactness of the flock by separating himself from his brother and father. The elder has been loyal and faithful. The younger was lost, but maybe wanted to be. The elder wants neat consequences. He has failed to recognize that all the father had was his. Both boys thereby stretch the integrity of the flock and pose different challenges for a shepherd to resolve. The reader is left uncertain as to whether the father can reconcile the flock now that they are proximally back together. Seems this is our invitation point: do we identify with the older brother, the younger, or the father?

Jesus begs us to reconsider what we do with the lost. God goes looking for them, even to the point of social, personal, and economic disgrace. God wants the integrity of the flock above all else; God can't stand to lose one. Of anything. Or anyone. God's approach is not practical, it is mystical. That does not mean it is illogical—meaning and richness are always deeper than reason. To God, sheep are not commodities, but children. We are invited to cultivate concern for the lost rather than condemnation for the prodigal. We are invited to celebrate God's saving grace.

42

Master

Luke 16:1–13

No one who cooperates in cheating the master would want to hire the steward—he's a proven thief! He doesn't cancel their bills, either, just diminishes them. The steward is commended for the same behavior that got him fired in the first place. Jesus advises that we use dishonest wealth to make friends, in direct contradiction to the gospel according to the Beatles: "Money Can't Buy Me Love." Jesus then tells the listener to be faithful with dishonest wealth: does that mean by being increasingly dishonest? He concludes with the one line that makes the most sense, but seems to be the most difficult to live into in our bones: no one can serve two masters.

Father Willy Crespo was a prison chaplain for several years in San Diego before becoming a parish priest. On a chance Sunday visit eight years ago, he shed some light on a parable that always confounded me. One year in prison ministry, the fiscal year-end was approaching and there were considerable funds left. He was advised, by the warden no less, to make sure he spent his apportioned money, lest his budget be decreased next year. So Willy ordered some built-in-bookshelves for the counseling room, shelves that would be useful, but that he would have had a difficult time justifying otherwise. They were custom-made and arrived in rather large crates, fully assembled. The counseling room was upstairs and neither the entry door nor the stairwell was particularly tall. Willy could not get the shelves to fit any way he tried. Enter convict Jack who told Willy that he needed four strong guys and three blankets; they could smuggle those shelves into the chapel just fine. He did. The very skill that earned Jack his sentence earned the chapel and counseling center new shelves.

Perhaps Jesus invites us to leave no skill or facet of ourselves unused in growing God's family. Crawfish boils. Plumbing. Knitting. We have become accustomed to the ministries of fellowship, groundskeeping, and prayer shawls. How might we use even more of our skills to smuggle things into the rooms of God's house that otherwise might not fit in?

Luke is questioning our dogged determination to bifurcate experiences and people into the categories of clean and unclean, sacred and secular, pure and dishonest. We often lose parts of ourselves in the name of propriety, and in the process we erect barriers to entering all the rooms in God's house, for ourselves and countless others. The liturgical tradition places a premium upon reverence in worship, yet one of my greatest joys in serving at the Lord's table was a verger who was never afraid to offer a joke when the opportunity arose, especially while washing my hands at the Eucharist. He opened doors to rooms in God's home I would never have let myself into. How sacred the mundane became.

Matthew's Jesus says that serving mammon is mutually exclusive with serving God. Mammon is success, money, and power all rolled into one. Luke insisted on "wealth" as more significant for us to hear than "mammon." Is it the wealth of the owner that makes him dismiss his steward without investigating the charges against him? Are some lives worth less than others? Does wealth ultimately lead us down the same rabbit hole as scarcity—never being or having enough?

Perhaps Luke is just writing to a group that is often caught up in costs and exchanges, and therefore hones in on the center of their idolatry. If so, what would Luke's Jesus say to us at this time in history? Can we serve God and politics at the same time? God and careers? God and uber-parenting? I believe the contrast in serving God and wealth still holds; we are easily distracted by the means over God's ends. In other words: idolatry. Whatever means you have, use them to enlarge the doors of God's rooms. Smuggle folks in if you need to. If God is truly everywhere all the time, then God must somehow be in both country and rap music, in math, and on stilts. Weave your life—both the honest and dishonest parts—into God's tapestry, and be the just steward who delights not only the master but the world.

43

Believing Is Seeing

Luke 16:19–31

This parable is particular to Luke. In it, there is a rich man, διυες in Greek, which is better translated "money-bags." Without a name, he is a bundle of possessions, a noble as evidenced by his purple wardrobe. In the ancient world, purple dye was produced by extracting the ink sac from a particular mollusk, indigenous off the coast of Tyre and Sidon (modern Lebanon), and was as valuable as gold itself. There were regulations against the nouveau riche wearing purple, akin to impersonating an officer. Minor nobility could wear a garment fringed in purple, but only a member of the ruling class could afford to be robed in purple. (Ever wonder where the bishop's purple comes from?) Then, there is Lazarus, "God has helped" in Hebrew, a poor man who begs outside of Money-bags's house, apparently with meager success. Jesus says nothing of the piety of either man, but only describes their economic state and their proximal relationship to one another. It is possible that Money-bags has never seen Lazarus; he undoubtedly has servants to do the errands and beggars were best ignored or avoided (then as now), lest they be encouraged or validated in their deserved status, laziness, or tendency to buy alcohol or drugs with food money.

The first surprise in the story is that there is a reversal of circumstances in the afterlife. Resurrection of the dead and immortality of the soul were both ideas in their infancy at the time of Luke's writing. Resurrection originated as an idea in Hebrew culture around the second century BCE from exposure to Persian and Greek philosophies and from the particular persecutions of the Seleucid King Antiochus IV Epiphanes. (Side note: Epiphanes can be translated "God made manifest." Jewish folk called him Epimanes, meaning "madness made manifest.") Antiochus effectively outlawed Judaism by banning circumcision (mothers of the circumcised had to wear the mutilated infants around their neck before meeting their own punishment), forbidding Torah possession and study (possessors were burned with their scrolls), and by sacrificing a pig to Zeus in the holy of holies (Daniel calls this the abomination that causes desolation). Guerilla resistance broke out against these policies by the family of Mattathias and his sons, especially under the leadership of Judas called Maccabeus ("the hammer"). One can read this story in the Apocryphal books of 1 and 2 Maccabees.

During the Maccabean revolt, when young men and women were losing their lives for practicing their faith, the idea of a physical resurrection entered Judaism: people whose lives were cut short would get their lives back so that they could fulfill the opportunities that had been denied them. Resurrection was not initially a spiritual idea, but rather restoration of life for the persecuted. Hell was also new. The Greeks had Hades, the place of the dead where some met ironic punishments, but, frankly, most just lingered in the dark (like Orpheus) under the ground. The Hebrews had Sheol, a similar place of the dead for all.

In this story from Luke, Lazarus does not go to heaven, but to Abraham's bosom. Wherever that is, Abraham's bosom is clearly preferable to Hades. No reason for this reversal is given: Money-bags gets what he eschewed and Lazarus gets what he could not have. If Jesus stopped here, we could read this as the ultimate overthrow of the proletariat by the bourgeois with divine sanction. But that's not the end of the story.

Money-bags seems to think he is still important, and Lazarus still a disposable peasant. Money-bags does not even bother speaking to Lazarus, but asks Abraham to send the beggar on errands: to offer him some water off of his finger or to appear to his family so that they will do something different, although it is not clear what. Will they give their money away? Stop banqueting each day? Look for vagrants? Abraham refuses because there is no crossing from his bosom to Hades and insists that people who do not believe what they have will not believe in what they do not have. This counterintuitive idea parallels mathematical proofs: laws require infinite occurrence, but are overturned by a single counterexample. Would a miracle trump all of our doubts for the rest of our lives or only momentarily? Do we fail to see God present in the world and in one another because God is absent or because our vision itself is to blame?

Seeing is believing, but in this story, believing is seeing. I had a pastoral care teacher whose final exam was a single question: name the person who cleans the building. Perhaps that was a little unfair since it wasn't in the study guide, but it was in the spirit of Luke. The fact that I bristled at this pedagogical move reveals something about my own way of seeing. Maybe Luke isn't giving us a window of revelation about eternity. Maybe he wants us to see the life we are missing now. We so often struggle to see God's grace because our eyes are just plain closed. Where might you open your eyes today and see a glimpse of God?

44

Flipped Prejudice

Luke 17:11–19

Remember the lesson of the Good Samaritan in Luke 10:25–37: there were no "good" Samaritans. Jesus's friends and audience would have been just as shocked by the gratitude of the SS Colonel for his Jewish healer or the Tutsi guerilla's appreciation for a Hutu. In chapter 32, I wondered if it was the inability of the Jewish man to refuse help from the object of his prejudice that allowed the entire story to work. This story rests on a similar axis.

Ten men with an icky skin blight seek a restoration of health and encounter Jesus. Hard to know if these ten had moved past the standard social and religious divisions with one another. When an outcast and a probable contagion, is one vector worse than another? They approach Jesus. They express their need. Jesus tells them to present themselves to the priests. Remember, priests were not religious experts or more pious than others; they did not complete a master's degree in ethics or pastoral care. Priests were butchers. They were also public health analysts. As public health reflected theological purity and sacrifices, priests had more than twice the apparent responsibility and more than twice the apparent authority—they could decide who was allowed to live and worship and have value in a community. It is likely that nine of the lepers will be heading south to Jerusalem to visit their priests while the Samaritan, being fundamentally unclean by southern Jewish standards, would need to head north to the shrine at Mt. Gerazim; the Jerusalem clergy would call him unclean regardless of his skin condition. All ten apparently trust Jesus to go to the examining chaplains, a fairly remarkable feat. They risk being rejected again, declared outcasts by possibly the same clerics that exiled them in the first place. But they all go. On the way, they are each healed of whatever malady lost them their communities in the first place. Presumably, the priests they visit will restore them to their previous community standing and their "healing" will be complete.

We have seen Jesus be generous with Samaritans before in both word and deed, so it is no surprise that he helps a Samaritan again, this time closer to Samaria and a distance away from Jerusalem to the south. For some reason, this Samaritan appears to be the only one of the ten to notice that he is healed on the way. Maybe the other nine had lesions on their backs they could not see or went to the priests not in faith, but in obedience. Perhaps the other nine didn't go at all, but left Jesus's presence in disappointment that he would ask them to go back to where their problems began in the first place. That would sure make the passage more coherent: if the Samaritan was the only one to risk reconciliation, his faith made him well. But we don't know that.

How far did he get before the Samaritan noticed he was healed? A few paces or several miles? Is Luke using this story to shame his audience: if a dirty old Samaritan is the only grateful one, how much more should clean people be thankful? Shaming others by making them feel fundamentally flawed creates enmity and codifies the shortcomings that are already ruling their lives, especially for lepers who are told that their illness is deserved. There is only healthy guilt (I made a bad decision), never healthy shame (I am bad). To be sure, the Samaritan shows gratitude, but he also models grateful living by noticing goodness and seeking reconciliation along the way instead of at the end. I could do this more often for sure. We often forget that the world is big and interconnected, that our hybrid batteries require metals only available in Africa, that much of our produce in Texas comes from Mexico, that the roads we rely on for work and leisure were built by the taxes we detest. We are not islands and we need one another.

What if this story is also an invitation to consider Jesus in a completely new way? What if Jesus is actually surprised that a Samaritan is grateful? John Wesley wrote that ignorance is not sin unless it is willful.[14] What if Jesus was raised to be prejudiced against Samaritans but never had the opportunity to question his upbringing until he came into contact with one? He'd be a great deal like us. What if he was without sin because he repented of his prejudice when confronted with cognitive dissonance? That, too, is a model for us.

A sacrament is an outward sign of an inward and spiritual grace. A sacrament is an opportunity to physically participate with God. Repentance following a new learning like this seems sacramental to me. I have recognized prejudices ingrained in me by my parents, town, and church. Some of them I have flipped and others I have proudly and foolishly held onto. What if this story is a reminder that we have opportunities each day to join Jesus in flipping our prejudices? We can certainly grow in gratitude with the Samaritan and grow in grace and sacramental learning with Jesus.

---

14. John Wesley, "The Wilderness State," *The Works of the Reverend John Wesley, A. M.* (Charleston, SC: Nabu Press, 2011), 415.

45

Persistence

Luke 18:1–8

Widows, along with children, were among the most vulnerable in the ancient world. Unable to possess property or own their income in the marketplace, widows were essentially goods, and damaged goods at that, without owners. Possessions of their deceased husbands, their choices were to go home to their parents (should they still be alive) and be reintroduced to economic hardship, belong to their deceased spouse's younger brother to produce a male son who will grow to replace their dead husband (Levirate marriage and the key to understanding the book of Ruth), beg, or prostitute themselves.

In this parable, a widow, the weakest in a community, pleads her case to the strongest, a judge. Most judges did not have courtrooms, but adjudicated cases at the city gate. As most peasants lived outside the city in an agrarian society, they entered cities for the sake of commerce and taxes; the gates were the shopping malls and bureaucratic centers. Judges were not necessarily schooled in case law, but tended to be the oldest (thirty-four at the time of Jesus was considered old) and most prosperous (goods were a sign of both wisdom and divine favor). It is difficult to tell whether judges were paid for their services; most likely not. Judicial posts were probably honorary and, therefore, judges belonged to the 1 percent.

In this story, the judge is unjust. He respects no one, not even God, and therefore might be as impartial as they come. A widow comes before him and pleads her case. We do not know if she is in the right; we just know that she is persistent. She shows up so frequently that she is about to wear the guy out (or even "give him a black eye" in some translations). Perhaps her low station leads people to assume that she is being denied justice. She comes so often and pleads so doggedly that it seems this judge begins to worry that he might lose honor by not deciding in her favor. Though he is impartial and perhaps knows that her case may not have merit, he grants her petition to save his own status. Jesus says that if people of the world function like this, giving into the pressure of persistence over maintaining impartiality and objectivity, how much more will God, who is just and compassionate, listen to our prayers.

A few thoughts come to mind regarding what we believe about the nature of God. After the golden calf incident, God plans to wipe out the people and start over with Moses (Exod. 32:1–14). Moses intervenes by pointing out this will damage God's reputation among the nations. After all, what sort of God frees a people from slavery only to slay them in the desert? It seems Moses persuades not through the people's merit or God's compassion, but through God's concern for honor. It is hard to accept that God would spare folk to avoid looking bad. Also, Moses models that prayer can change God's mind. We often pray "your will be done" lest we sound too pushy, but ask for the same thing over and over. Surely we do hope God will heal our sick friend or help our house sell. Is prayer like this? Do we need to prick God's conscience to get results? Do we need to prove our perseverance, as the parable of the widow could imply? Or does the fact that God is just and compassionate, unlike the judge, mean we shouldn't read it that way? Perhaps prayer is more about a constant awareness of God's presence—an awareness that shapes our interactions with others, the world, and what will be best indeed.

Ninety percent of success is just showing up. Maybe Jesus is encouraging apparently powerless people to keep showing up, regardless of the obvious lack of global tide-turning? If we keep throwing starfish into the sea, will we change both the beach and the waters? Will evil and slander and shame and all the isms of our world disappear if we continue to resist them? Surely it's worth a try! Perseverance in God's case might just overturn indifference if we keep showing up.

God spoke first. God said, "Let us create humankind in our image." What if prayer is not about asking God for what we want or trying to bend God's will toward our own notions of justice, but answering God? How do we respond? With indifference or consideration? With objectivity or with subjectivity? How do our lives answer God's assertion that all of creation is "very good"?

Luke and Jesus both assure us that God is not like this judge. Which makes me wonder why I spend most of my spiritual life praying submissively instead of boldly, locked into notions that there are better ways to pray than others, and that it is my Christian duty to ask God to save the lost. Luke suggests that God isn't just interested in saving the lost, but is actively looking for them, with God's constant, curious, compassionate presence.

46

As a Child

Luke 18:9–17

In this all-too-familiar story, we recognize the proverbial message: the Pharisee is a hypocrite and the tax collector is sincere. However, the original audience would have been shocked by this story. Pharisees were very serious about living into worship, study, outreach, and morality. Many prayers from the time of Jesus read just like the one he quotes. Many of my own do. I am so grateful I am not an addict. I am glad that I do not have a prison record or college debts. I am appreciative that I have all of my limbs, and an intact nuclear family. If I rank myself by these blessings, I miss the point, but I am grateful for them.

Tax collectors were generally perceived as rogues and extortionists who abused their religion, and relationships. This particular tax collector goes home cleansed that day, but imagine that he does the same bit every day, lives down to the Pharisee's stereotype, and never changes. Would the tax man go home justified then, if his contrition never amended his life? Humility, after all, is not about self-deprecation, but being exactly who we are before God, no more, but also no less. The Pharisee probably describes himself accurately: he likely does tithe and fast weekly and neither steals nor commits adultery. It is one thing to resist a stereotype and another to impose it. Maybe this is where he and we so often go wrong. As my dad so often said, "The minute you think you are different from everyone else is the minute you are just like everyone else."

Enter the kids, standing on shakier ground than even tax collectors. At the time of Jesus, children were not doted upon. They had no rights and were chattel. They took resources to raise and were unable to return the investment for at least ten years. Infant mortality was extremely high; some scholars suggest that children at the time had a 50 percent chance of survival to age thirteen.[15] So Jesus likely stuns his disciples when he says that the kingdom of God belongs to people with no rights, power, or advocates, who are deeply beset with a struggle to make it ten years. They could not understand this and I am pretty sure this remains a head-scratcher.

How *do* children receive the kingdom of God? Is it their ability to believe in the unseen? It is not uncommon for children to have a strong sense of God's presence and pray conversationally with God out loud. Maybe it is because children are undaunted by paradox and cognitive dissonance? Perhaps, in Lukan fashion, children are much more capable and quick to accommodate their worldview around new information than adults, who tend to assimilate new information? Children also seem much more quick to admit they were wrong or at least to make up and move on.

Perhaps Jesus is not asking us to receive the kingdom of God as a child does, but to receive the kingdom as we would receive a child. We have automatic patience with children (well, most of us do, anyway), because we don't ascribe motives to their inability to feed themselves or complete tasks without supervision. We usually remember, even when frustrated, that children do not have the emotional resources to cope with a series of challenges or exhaustion and we actually expect children to takes risks and fail, to make mistakes. When a child cries, we usually try and figure out what is wrong or where a caregiver is, even if we do not know the child.

What if we cared for the kingdom of God like it were a child? More specifically, what if we looked at each and every person as God's child, God's little bitty baby, in need of care and nurture? What if we were patient

---

15. Meyers, *Rediscovering Eve*, 98.

with folks when they were at their wit's end? What if, instead of casting shame or judgment or projecting intent, we looked to comfort or find a caregiver for someone who failed? What if we encouraged risk-taking in adults, especially around grace, and affirmed messiness as an essential part of participating in anything? What if we could look at the family member who has made a scene at the last nine family gatherings, the colleague who is habitually grumpy, the guy who cut the Starbucks line, as cranky, hungry, in need of comfort? What if Jesus is asking us to have compassion for adults, especially ones we know, like we would children?

And what if we looked at ourselves as children of God, especially in our weakness and frailty? What if we were able to perceive in the mirror a beautiful baby of God that needs nurture, even when we are ashamed or angry? Could we care for ourselves as we would a precious child, patiently and compassionately, appreciatively and thoughtfully? (After all, I don't know many folks who plan on ruining things for themselves and others when they make a mistake. Even if they do, sounds like some tantrums I have seen possess small children.) Could we dare to love greater, suspend anger to care and see the need behind any perceived disrespect? What would the world be like if it were loved and received as a child?

Insight

Luke 19:1–10

Contrary to popular expectations, Zacchaeus may not have been a "wee little man." He certainly was rich. Luke gives us that irrefutably. He was also a tax collector. The ancient connection is that he was a cheat, a used-car salesman of the worst kind. He sold his own people and their future to Rome, to paganism, to uncleanliness. He was too rich and complicit with the empire to be touched, but not too big to be boxed out by a crowd who had to live with him. Jesus did not have to be a prophet to know who Zacchaeus was, or to realize that the people of Jericho did not even want him to see Jesus; their body language, his clothing, and their likely murmuring against him would have made all of that clear.

In many ways, this is a parallel story to the blind man in Luke 18:35–43. There is a man who would like to see Jesus and a crowd gets in the way. However, Zacchaeus's blindness is not strictly physical. Taking matters into his own hands, he climbs a tree. Wearing a dress and a nail apron as underwear, he exposes himself to the very people who he has exposed and potentially defrauded. Jesus sees him, but not as the rest of Jericho does. What does Jesus see? A project? Someone to save? Or is it someone whom God loves just as he is, in all of his uncertainty and brokenness? Jesus will stay with him.

Scandal. Jesus will stay with a sinner and a traitor. Jesus will not only meet the ayatollah and the Shah, but recognize their humanity, accept their hospitality, and be beholden to them. Jesus doesn't seem to know any better. Zacchaeus, touched by Jesus's compassion, either gains or regains his sight. He publicly repents and gives half of what he owns to the have-nots with generous interest—think reparations.

Zacchaeus has finally seen Jesus and therefore changes. Because Jesus's favor is not at stake and there is no longer a risk of rejection from God, Zacchaeus is free to be generous, to be profligate with grace, to be exactly who he was made to be.

And so salvation comes not only to Zacchaeus, but to his house. Zacchaeus has been saved from his blindness. He has seen Jesus as Jesus is and realigned his life and practices. Economically, his household will suffer from the extremely generous pledge of repentance. But they will have him as his whole self, perhaps for the first time ever. Jesus came not for the found, but for the lost. May we make room for others to see Jesus. May we, like Zacchesus, host Jesus in our homes as a guest. May we publicly repent when we are wrong for the sake of our lost selves.

48

Be the Opposition

Luke 19:11–27

Luke frames this parable with an explanation of how Jesus is confronting expectations: how, when, and where the kingdom of God is going to appear. An absentee nobleman goes off to climb the status ladder. The locals send a counterdelegation. Absentee landlords have always been an issue. The locals lose in the story. They often do. Jesus's listeners would have been familiar with this scenario.

Originally from Idumea, the family of Herod the Great ("great" being self-conferred) were forcibly converted to Judaism by the Hasmoneans around 137 BCE. Herod took leadership against the previous emperor, Octavian, in favor of Antony after the death of Julius Caesar. He backed the wrong horse and begged Octavian to keep him in place, citing his loyalty to Antony through rise and fall. It was a virtue he would transfer to Augustus Caesar. The people of Idumea sent a delegation to oppose Herod. Octavian ignored them, crowned Herod anew, and Herod slaughtered his opponents. Herod had a great number of children and killed half of them, leading Augustus to quip, "It is better to be Herod's pig than son."[16] Herod, like George Foreman, named each of his children after himself.

---

16. Macrobius, *Saturnalia*, 2:4:11

After Herod's death in 4 BCE, his kingdom was divided among his three surviving sons. Archelaus Herod ruled Judea, having recently overseen the building of a palace in Jericho and aqueducts in the area. His first act was to slaughter three thousand people. The three Herods had to journey to Rome to receive their official titles. The Idumeans sent a delegation to opposed Archelaus. They begged for a different ruler. They lost with the concession that Archelaus would be their "ethnarch" until he earned their affection and kinship. He returned with authority and put his opponents to wretched ends. Jesus most likely gave an apt description of these events to the crowd today as their messianic anticipations climaxed. There were three different responses to the power-grabbing noble: servitude, paralysis, and opposition.

Servitude. While away, the noble entrusted quite a bit of money to some slaves. The first turns a *mina*, approximately $33,000, into $330,000. A bumper rate of return by any standard. He will not keep the money, of course, but will be rewarded with responsibility over ten cities in the new kingdom. He does not get less work, he gets more. The second turned his $33,000 into $165,000. Again, ahead of market rates in any lifetime. He will rule five cities, not five minas. We don't know the reward for failure, but we do know that faithfulness begets more responsibilities.

Paralysis. The third servant returns the $33,000. He was worried about transaction fees, market trends, and the lack of anything like the FDIC. He could have been robbed and there were neither ATMs, ATM cameras, nor police forces. He buries the money—the safety deposit box of the ancient world—and returns the principle completely intact. Please note, there is no loss to the investor. He was afraid to lose, afraid that he could not reap where he did not sow, afraid that interest only would not be enough, that his master was not going to be satisfied whatever.

It is easy to judge this particular servant poorly. If he was afraid, why did he seal his own fate with his inactivity? The master says the same. Perhaps it is because he was paralyzed by shame instead of motivated by guilt. Guilt is the feeling that one made a bad choice. Guilt is highly correlated with success as guilt implies agency, an ability to try again. Shame is a feeling of failure in the self, that there is something fundamentally flawed. Without agency, there is really no point in trying again because things could get worse, not better. The third servant is so paralyzed by fear that he cannot serve. I wish there was a fourth servant who invested their mina and lost it. I wonder if the master would be happy for the try or even more dissatisfied. What we do know is that the one who is afraid to act in his master's absence loses what little he had. While the mina was never his anyway, it was in his charge. Perhaps his problem is with his vision; the servant does not understand his master.

Opposition. A wretched end for the enemies, slaughtered in front of the new monarch. Contrast this against the traditional analogy of Jesus as the absent noble and humanity as the servants. What if Jesus is, once again, trying to overcome the imagination of his most zealous supporters by describing the reality of business as usual? If he has come to institute an earthly kingdom, there will be reprisals. Loyalists will be rewarded with even greater responsibilities. Those who want an immediate change of leader are missing the opportunity to change the entire system. Yesterday's conclusion might be today's thesis: Jesus came to seek and save the lost, not to punish his opponents as Herod and Archelaus had just done, not to place paralyzing demands on those lucky enough to stay alive, not to levy shame upon God's family. Read this way, Jesus might be asking if this is what we really want—more of the same rigged and cruel game?

An analogy for today might be theologian and philosopher Mary Daly and her push beyond the feminism of the 1970s. The world would not be righted when women were in power. Rather, she believed the world would be righted when power was equally distributed, when lordship itself was laid aside, when access to justice was equally available. God does not aim for another iteration of oppression. It is hard to say who the heroes are in the story—the opposition that ultimately fails? The servants who hustle for worthiness to please a seemingly implacable master? The servant who does not profit an apparently awful man? Jesus might well be understood as the opposition (especially on Palm Sunday) to the Roman Empire, a dissenter who will be crushed (on Friday). Where are we in the story and, wherever that is, are we content to recycle the *Games of Thrones* or elect to change the rules and even the game itself?

Symbolic Resistance

Luke 19:28–44

In their book *The Last Week*, Marcus Borg and John Dominic Crossan tell in great detail about a different procession into Jerusalem on Palm Sunday, the procession that Luke, Mark, and Matthew all leave out: the military parade of Pontius Pilate from the north in Caesarea Maritima to the temple mount in Jerusalem, an area the size of three football fields, dominated by a towering citadel with a view of the temple courts.[17] Pilate preferred the cosmopolitan city of Caesarea most of the year, coming to Jerusalem only for the volatile holy days. Pilate arrived clothed in purple, legionnaires marching in unison bearing their standards. (According to the Talmud, standards were idolatrous, and represented the veneration of Roman power.) All to remind the swell of pilgrims—likely 400,000 people (a hundred times the normal population)—that they had in fact already been conquered, and that celebrating the Jewish holy days was a privilege to appreciate, not an opportunity to foment revolt.

Jesus comes from the north, riding on a donkey. Folks welcome him with their cloaks, a rabble red carpet. How many? We have no idea. The parade route? Just opposite the temple, passing through the Kidron Valley,

---

17. John Dominic Crossan and Marcus Borg, *The Last Week: What the Gospels Really Teach about Jesus's Final Days in Jerusalem* (New York: HarperOne, 2007).

lies the Mount of Olives, the start of the procession. Because the valley is saddle-shaped and relatively open, Jesus's journey would have been evident to many, including the newly arrived Roman garrison. The donkey is a curious choice. When David conquered Jerusalem from the Jebusites, the first Hebrew to do so, he rode into the conquered city victorious on a donkey. At the time of David, Hebrews had not discovered how to saddle or bridle a horse (that did not happen until after 722 BCE); they failed to recognize that a horse breathes solely through its nose while oxen and donkeys breathe solely through their mouths. Putting a bit in a donkey's mouth invites suffocation, but not so a horse. Riding a donkey is actually a military disadvantage; donkeys are not particularly tall, spry, fast, or agile. Therefore, David's mount was a symbol of peace; the victory had already been won. By the time of Jesus, one would have expected a horse for a contender, a large one at that. Perhaps even one of Hannibal's African elephants. The crowd seems to understand Jesus's donkey ride as Davidic expectation: another Jewish kingdom, free from Rome, and a conqueror who could, as David did, succeed in Jerusalem where so many others had failed.

Perhaps this is why Jesus picked a donkey: it was an antisymbol to Pilate's jockeying for power and it revealed Jesus's deep faith that God's victory is assured. Because of this depth of faith, Jesus did not need to use symbols of war or rivalry, but was able to deploy tactics of repentance and challenge that normally presuppose a power base. (Three to six years after the crucifixion, Judas the Galilean, another donkey rider at the Samaritan holy place on Mount Gerazim, was butchered along with several hundred followers by the same Pontius Pilate. Pilate was ultimately removed from his position following this.) It is also a challenge to the efficacy of coercive and dominating means in general and makes us wonder how we might treat others in conflict if our trust in God's kin-dom were secure.

Riding into Jerusalem on a donkey is like standing in front of a tank in China's Tiananmen Square armed with a briefcase; marching to Birmingham while being sprayed by firehoses, or publicly burning Indian registration cards in apartheid South Africa. Where did these prophets find the faith and courage to engage in symbolic and real resistance, knowing their lives were in jeopardy? Surely God is calling us to show faith in God's way, to apologize openly when we are wrong and seek reconciliation, to think about how our everyday choices step on or with others. Maybe God is calling us to expand the invitation we get every Sunday at the Eucharist for all to join God at God's table by making sure people have tables and the means to get to them. Maybe Palm Sunday is a simple reminder that Jesus chose a different way from force and domination and that we can too, as parents, churchgoers, workers, citizens, and friends.

The Pharisees seem to understand all of the above and ask Jesus to rebuke the crowd for praising him instead of God. Jesus refuses—the stones will cry out in praise if people do not. The heavens themselves are conspiring to the greatness of God and we are invited to join them, or miss out, to our detriment.

In what is likely a post-70 CE addition to Luke, the year in which General Trajan not only looted Jerusalem but burned the temple to the ground, Jesus laments that the people object to his procession of peace and seem all too enthralled with Pilate's tour de force. If only Jerusalem, the "city of peace," had known which things make for peace, its little ones could have been gathered instead of scattered, its temple a nest for all nations, instead of a den for robbers.

The ways of peace are hidden from eyes that are not physiologically myopic, but theologically myopic. Sometimes we are so committed to efficacy and efficiency that we write off diplomacy, especially in our relationships, let alone our politics. If only we could have seen the ways that lead to peace. It is not too late for us; it only gets harder. God's emissaries are all around us, calling us to ride on donkeys instead of war horses. God's universe conspires to hail the reconciliation of God's presence and we are invited to lay down our cloaks for the parade today.

Authority

Luke 20:1-8

This passage from Holy Week sets the scene for all that is to unfold afterwards. The authorities, the ones with the backing of the Roman government, have seen Jesus act against the temple and Rome. Jesus questioned *their* authority as well as Rome's and they ask where his authorization to probe their authority comes from. Of course, we all know it comes from God, but power has never really appreciated hearing that answer. Remember, these are religious authorities themselves, with the weight of tradition on their side. Divine injunction is dangerous precisely because they have the power to stone Jesus as a heretic (while crucifixion was a capital punishment controlled by Rome, the local authorities had the ability to settle their own matters). Jesus has more he wants to do and thus avoids the confrontation the authorities hope he will take by turning the tables.

In the teachings that follow, the theme remains: Jesus is put on the defensive by the authorities, who are looking for an excuse to eliminate him and the threats to their influence. In each case, Jesus does more than parry their offense, he goes on the attack himself and offers us extremely pithy and vexing teachings about money, power, and resurrection.

The authorities all of sudden find themselves worried about, well, authority. If they discount John by identifying his authority as human, they lose their authority from the people who found value in John's ministry and undoubtedly appreciated his ability to challenge power. If they celebrate John by declaring his authority as divinely inspired, they lose their authority from Rome and the government that backs their authority in the first place, but also cut John's head off. The authorities all of a sudden cannot speak with conviction, and, of course, will lose no matter what they say now. "We don't know" is not the kind of answer that one wants to hear from those in charge. Tally: Jesus 1, authorities < 0. It is inspiring to see Jesus foil his adversaries.

But perhaps this exchange is more than just verbal defense-turned-offense and a lesson in what savvy social skills can do for you in even the harshest of circumstances. Authority is built on respect within relationships. I excel at criticizing ideas, but need to grow into the discipline of appreciating the context and potential contribution of ideas.

Questioning someone's credentials, while sometimes helpful, can also be a very convenient way to dismiss them. Labels can all too often flatten or over categorize. Oh, you're a Democrat? Your opinion doesn't matter. You grew up Baptist? You should be grateful we let you serve in the Episcopal Church. How often we quickly dismiss someone on the basis of authority. Are people worth the time to listen to, even if we know we will disagree? Why are we so afraid? We might be surprised. We may find a piece of God in their humanity.

51

Eternity

Luke 20:27–40

There was a rich diversity in Judaism at the time of Jesus. The Sadducees, Pharisees, and Essenes all recognized the primacy of the Torah for guidance. All three believed in fidelity in worship and strict adherence to priestly codes. The Sadducees, who do not believe in an afterlife, come up with a trap, possibly referencing a story in Tobit, a book in the Apocrypha, which describes a woman who has been widowed six times. The Sadducees want Jesus to determine to whom the woman will belong in this supposed afterlife. After all, women belonged to their husbands and she had been married seven times.

Jesus has a rather interesting reply: people don't belong to each other in resurrected life, only in the life we choose to live now, which is something less than what God intends for us. I believe Jesus is saying that people will not be commodities when God's imagination plays out. He might be inviting us to live a life even now that is free from objectification, not only in obvious ways such as human trafficking, but through marginalizing others because of homelessness, mental illness, incarceration, disagreeing with us, and so on. If there are no slaves in heaven, why would we settle for them on earth?

Jesus then says something quite pithy about God: people who have died on earth are not dead in God. God does not say, "I was the God of

Abe, Ike, and Jake," but "I AM." In Hebrew, the phrase really means "I was, am, and will be all at the same time." In the Lord, life is not ended, but changed. Eternal life and eternal love are about choosing to practice loving justice, mercy, and dignity. We should not be stingy with forgiveness because God is not stingy. Jesus urges us to turn to the Life that wants to Live in us.

Once more, Jesus turns a trap into an opportunity to engage in a holy conversation. So can we.

52

Dignity over Piety

Luke 20:45–21:3

Jesus warns of practicing piety in order to climb the heavenly pyramid. Jesus is challenging us to grow from a love of people and God, rather than compete with one another for limited resources of divine favor; to pray because God already approves of us rather than to pray to earn God's approval.

In the traditional version of the story, Jesus lauds the generosity of a poor widow because she gives everything she has to God. Or was it her willingness to give that is lauded; the widow's mite is the widow's might? Or are God's judgments relative: God looks not at the amount, but the cost we bear, which is variable? This invites the thought that God examines not just our deeds, but our motives, passions, and biases. In *Dare to Lead*, Brené Brown concludes that the single most determining factor in whether or not we live joyful lives is whether or not we believe that other people, especially when they do wrong, are doing the best they can with what they have.[18]

However, I think Jesus had a different meaning in mind, one connected to the condemnation of the scribes in the story that precedes the widow's mite. In order to receive welfare from the temple, widows had to

---

18. Brown, *Dare to Lead*, 213–17.

be completely penniless. They could have nothing except the clothes on their back. This woman, without resources, is not just putting some coins in the collection plate, she is putting her self-sufficiency and dignity in it so that she can have a chance of survival. She is courageously offering her last to a system that demands it in order to assist her. The scribes, who made this rule to make sure no one was cheating the temple, have forced this woman into giving her last bit of currency to get help. They are condemned for taking not only her dignity in the name of charity, but also her hope of sustainability or independence. How similar are we today when we worry that people are getting charity they don't really need, haven't had to work for, or don't deserve?

Even though God has unlimited resources, we do not. Every church I have been a part of has a "pastoral needs" fund. Episodically, word seems to get out that these funds can help with rent and utilities. How to evaluate which requests were truly worthy with limited funds available? Pastors often give after listening to stories sadder than I could contrive, and try to connect people with financial counseling and other resources in the community, always wishing more could be done while also wondering about what will happen with the aid given. This is exactly why handing out nonperishable meals are so popular: they allow us to give to the self-identified hungry with more dignity and generosity and less fear. I have even had parishioners tell me that giving away bags made them change their vision, from trying not to see the hungry to actively looking for them.

Some people worry about welfare systems creating systemic poverty and poor people having better insurance than folks who work full-time. When I fostered a child, the state provided Medicare. It was supposed to cover his needs as a "ward of the state." In reality, it often offered a single provider within a fifty-mile radius, or a provider who had stopped taking Medicare years ago, or one who was even deceased. Once, the benefit was turned off because we got him a social security number, as we had been told to do. I had to go to the office with my son and my three-month-old daughter on my day off. I waited an hour in a crowded room just to see an intake specialist. She told me to go to another building next door. I went. They told me, thirty minutes later, to go across town to a different office.

Hardly the luxury life I had heard so much about. How do we relieve the burdens of poverty without sapping the dignity out of the very folks we want to help raise up? *Toxic Charity* asks even more probing questions about how we can transition from hand-outs to hands-up and do this without being paralyzed as givers.[19]

How much dignity do people have to sacrifice to earn our forgiveness or trust in a second (or fifteenth) chance? Does our piety connect us more and more with people who live on the margins, or leave us more and more divided? Do we make people come to church before we help them? If people are not excited to receive Vienna Sausages from us, are we harsh or judgmental or are we okay with that, even if we have nothing else to offer? I usually figure that folks who get gifts from me are accountable for how they receive them; I am accountable for whether and how I give them. These include not only checks or food and medical supplies, but human resources of forgiveness and more chances.

19. Robert D. Lupton, *Toxic Charity: How Churches and Charities Hurt Those They Help, and How to Reverse It* (New York: HarperOne, 2012).

53

Fuel for the Journey

Luke 22:1–30

The chief priests and scribes are afraid of the very people they are meant to represent. 1 John 4:18 offers an insightful corrective to such representation: "Perfect love casts out fear (NRSV)." Precisely because they do not love the people they are called to represent before God, they scheme. Meanwhile, slander and accusation have taken hold of Judas and, in his fear, he does something that he will certainly regret soon after—he betrays Jesus.

Luke quickly moves to the story of the first Eucharist, also called the Last Supper. Luke is careful to set Jesus's last meal as the Passover meal (John sets it the day before Passover and has Jesus crucified as the lambs are being slaughtered). Passover is one of the holiest festivals in Judaism. The Passover meal described in Exodus and Deuteronomy is filled with reminders about the bondage in Egypt: bitter herbs, to reconnect to the bitterness of slavery, dipped in salt water (to represent tears.); matzah, because the dough did not have time to rise before the people fled. Bread and wine are blessed as they are every Shabbat.

Jesus blesses the bread and breaks it, but says that it is to be eaten as his body. The cup of wine is to be drunk as his blood. Undoubtedly, the disciples were just as confused as the Reformation theologians. Is this cannibalism? Do we reenact Jesus's sacrifice at the Eucharist? Without answering these questions, Luke has set up a system of meaning within the context of Passover. I am certain the Eucharist is mysterious enough and big enough to hold multiple meanings, but Luke focuses on strength for the journey. Lambs were not killed as substitutionary sacrifices; they were converted into calories and nutrition just before a long journey by people who ate meat only sporadically. Priests do not slaughter Passover lambs in Exodus, families do. Blood is the symbol of life force in the Bible, and could not be consumed, lest people thought they were imbibing the life force of the animal (its *chi*). That belonged to God and was to be poured out on the ground to return the life force to God. On Passover it went round the doorframe, signifying trust in God's deliverance.

In Luke, Jesus says that God stands poised to deliver us from the bondage of our pharaohs and to nourish us for the journey that will require the life force of Jesus. Whenever we eat wine and bread, we are to remember Jesus's life and teachings and be nourished to follow him as he leads us. We need this often. God nourishes not just our bodies at the Eucharist, but especially our spirits.

Judas was there. He and Jesus both seemed to know of the pending betrayal. Peter was there and would deny Jesus within hours. Jesus did not sacrifice Judas on an altar of righteousness or exclude Peter for having too little faith or improper discipleship. God's table is open to all. At the table we break bread and connect with one another. Perhaps we sacrifice our greater-than-thou-ness to eat at God's table, or perhaps we sacrifice our feelings of unworthiness to be there. God invites us to be nourished for our faith journey with the life and love of Jesus and to invite others to this incredible source of nutrition for the journey into a land God continued to promise, even on Saturdays and even with traitors.

I knew the Episcopal Church could be a spiritual home for me the first time I came to the altar rail in East County, San Diego. I had just left a church job and was there to heal in solitude. To my right was a well-to-do and gracious elderly woman wearing communion gloves and pearls. To my left was a refugee from Burma, veiled for the rail and barely able to speak English. To her left was a homeless man who may have been more interested in the coffee hour snacks than anything else. And we all knelt at God's table, sacrificed our carefully constructed roles and norms about sharing dinner vessels with strangers, and were nourished at God's table as equals.

The disciples do not debate Jesus's words with theological discourse on the nature of the meal, but with their constant worry about who will be the greatest in God's kingdom. Jesus tells them, for the one hundredth time, that the greatest is not the one with the most positional power, but the one with the most earned authority, the one who invites people into the family that know they do not belong and simultaneously convinces "the established family" that the outsiders do, in fact, belong. I rarely feel belonging for myself, let alone for others I can all too easily critique. That is why I need strength for the journey, as often as it is available. May we be nourished at the table by the life force of Jesus as often as we eat and drink so we can be nourishment to a hungry world and be willing to sacrifice our proud divisions on the altar of the Lord.

54

Weapons of Righteousness

Luke 22:31–38

The accuser and slanderer, Satan/the devil, would sift Simon like wheat, separate the chaff of his faith from the kernels. The difference between the accuser and John the Baptist, both of whom use the image of the threshing floor, is that the accuser would convince us to focus on the chaff instead of the kernel: we are chaff. The Baptist, on the other hand, would sift us like wheat in preparation for God's coming into our lives so that we can focus on the kernels.

Jesus knows that Peter's faith will fail. Three is a complete number, so it is hard to know whether Jesus is predicting precision or the fact that Peter will crumple at adversity. Either way, after this failure of faith, will Peter continue to wallow in a failure of faith and character: will he commit to the chaff, or will he repent, learn, and grow into the kernels that Jesus saw from the beginning? Will he have an existential crisis and be paralyzed, or take a second wind from the Holy Spirit to return and strengthen his siblings with him? We know that Peter will do the second, not the first. And doesn't Jesus invite us to do the same? When the cock crows, will we rejoice in the God of second chances or droop before the god of perfection? Roosters are meant to rouse us, not to judge or destroy us after all.

Jesus goes on. When you went out in vulnerability, you were cared for. When you took off your armor and notions of being completely self-sufficient and accepted your interdependence on others, you not only survived, you thrived. You saw the accuser fall like lightning from a place of prominence and influence as high as the sky. When they produce two swords; Jesus says it is enough. I wish Luke had added some inflection here so that I knew whether Jesus was rolling his eyes because the guys misunderstood him again or if he was genuinely satisfied with two swords among twelve people.

Perhaps Jesus is suggesting that should we be denied interdependence and counted among the lawless as so many others have before us, we will need to use our resources and connections carefully. Martin Luther King Jr. challenged the system by using weapons of righteousness and resistance to attack barriers to equality and justice. He was counted among the lawless. He lost his life without wielding a sword. I wonder if Jesus isn't asking us to use our resources to expose our common need for trust and mutuality toward the very people that seem the most threatening to us. How do we work to grant trust and second chances to those whom we count among the lawless?

The accuser would sift us like wheat. Jesus prayed for us to not only prevail by focusing on the kernels of grace and godliness within us instead of the chaff, but by repenting and strengthening our siblings, especially when they seem to be our enemies.

55

Reptilian Choices

Luke 23:13–25

Pilate is not a religious teacher nor a Jewish sympathizer. He does not bring Jesus's religious claims to trial, but investigates whether Jesus opposed taxation and the lordship of Caesar enough to threaten the continued dominance of Rome in Judea. Pilate concludes Jesus is not a threat. He will have Jesus flogged and release him. Why beat a man found not guilty? Because the legal system never declares anyone innocent, just "not guilty" given the evidence presented.

Beatings in the ancient world were stern warnings and anyone investigated was procedurally tortured. Ancients believed that taking people to the edge helped their ability to tell the truth. Inquiry did not happen during torture, but afterwards. It was, therefore, a serious event to be charged of a crime against the state and to be "examined." We read of this often in the Acts of the Apostles (also authored by Luke) where apostles are repeatedly beaten ahead of any formal inquiry. We don't know if the Sanhedrin took Jesus to the edge during the night or if the torturers had already had their way with Jesus. Either way, to face accusation is to go to the edge, which might explain how Satan and the devil became powers personified.

Our reptilian brains respond to accusation and slander in the same way that they respond to a lion or a rattlesnake. Cognitively, we haven't evolved to differentiate a physical threat from a social one. An accusation takes

147

us to the edge of our humanity: to our flight, fight, or freeze response, to adrenaline instead of serotonin. The crowd goes over the edge, Jesus does not. The crowd chooses vengeance, even death, for someone who does not meet their expectations and fantasy, for someone who challenges their insecure values. Pilate goes over the edge in the Gospels, submitting to a crowd of people he neither respects nor cares about, a crowd that could not have been large in size or influence. This sham trial and senseless accusation is an invitation to reflect on how often, when brought to the edge by accusation or criticism, we jump over with glee and without remorse.

The Gospels tell another peculiar custom of Pilate's—releasing a prisoner of their choice for the Passover. Not only does this contradict Pilate's known character, but such a practice defies common sense. Why would any government release a known insurrectionist in order to appease a mob during the most politically and religiously volatile time of the year? To do so would be tantamount to either abdication or the deepest possible hubris. There is no historicity of this practice, so why do the Gospel writers include it? It is a powerful commentary on the crowd. In Aramaic, Barabbas means "son of the father." In each of the four Gospels, the crowd picks the wrong son of the wrong father, preferring a murderer and insurrectionist to God's Messiah. Given a chance, would we prefer to forgive and be reconciled with Osama bin Laden, Hilary Clinton, or Donald Trump, or would we pick Barabbas as well?

Barabbas is about living in our reptilian past instead of our humanity. Barabbas represents tribalism. Barabbas is about refusing to learn, listen, reconsider, or empathize. And the Gospel writers knew how often we prefer and pick Barabbas over Jesus. But we don't have to.

56

Extraordinariness

Luke 23:26–56

More than any other Gospel writer, Luke emphasizes Jesus's extraordinary presence on Friday over any extraordinary pain. Unlike Mark, where Jesus dies with a loud cry after quoting Psalm 22's haunting first line, "My God, my God, why have you forsaken me?" Luke's Jesus commends his last breath—his spirit—to God and exhales. Unlike Matthew, Luke's Jesus does not thirst upon the cross, but offers paradise to the insurrectionist who repents. Luke's Jesus beseeches God's forgiveness for his executioners and mockers; they don't really know what they are doing, they don't really understand the scriptures, the Messiah, or Jesus.

This may be the myth of redemptive violence, that two wrongs can make something right, that Satan can cast out Satan. Whether or not they deserve rebuke, punishment, or condemnation, Jesus intercedes for them with God, with himself, for us. They are doing the best they can with what they have.

Brené Brown's research indicates that empathy requires such a perspective: other people are doing the best they can with what they have.[20] Empathy invites our consideration of the burdens that others bear instead of judgment

20. Cf. Brown, *Dare to Lead*, 213–17.

over the burdens themselves or how they are carried. This is extraordinary, like the prayer found at the Ravensbruck Concentration Camp:

> O Lord, remember not only the men and women of goodwill, but also those of ill will. But do not remember all the suffering they have inflicted upon us. Remember the fruits we bought, thanks to this suffering: our comradeship, our loyalty, our humility, the courage, the generosity, the greatness of heart which has grown out of this; and, when they come to judgement, let all the fruits that we have borne be their forgiveness. Amen.[21]

Extraordinary presence. Extraordinary hope. Extraordinary perseverance. This is Jesus on Friday. The women of Jerusalem, who have financed his ministry and sat at his feet as disciples, are the first to cry for his suffering. Jesus asks them not to. Extraordinary. He directs them to be prepared for the siege, destruction, and desolation of Jerusalem that will bring the collateral damages of starvation, sickness, fire, and unbridled reprisals. Weep for the future women and children who will be victims of war.

Even on the way to his death, Jesus invites us to contemplate his death in a way that expands our awareness of senseless violence and sin throughout the world so that we might have a connection with those in Sudan, Yemen, or the next town over and then do something about it. The mockery: save yourself. Jesus's extraordinariness is that he considers others alongside himself. Here is no messiah, but The Messiah. Jesus offers his spirit, his breath, and life force to God because no one else around seemed to want it. We are invited to breathe it in, especially on dark days.

In Matthew, the centurion identifies Jesus as either the son of God or the son of a god. In Luke, the centurion concludes that Jesus was innocent. Luke wants us to be innocent so that we can be what was in Matthew's mind: children of God.

The insurrectionists to his left and right ("thieves" is a poor translation) offer alternate orientations toward Jesus. It's odd how even the

---

21. Jo Bailey Wells, "Prayer for the Week," *Church Times*, November 2006, https://www.churchtimes.co.uk/articles/2004/16-january/faith/prayer-for-the-week.

damned jockey for position. These two have tried to overthrow Rome with their hatred and violence and have failed. One asks Jesus to save himself and them to prove he is the Messiah. Ironic, as this person does not seem to weigh himself, his own failed messianic actions, by his own words. Or maybe he does. Maybe he does what we do—lash out in our own failure toward others because its weight is too much for us to bear alone. He could not bring about his reign over others, and we similarly fail, because domination can never bring intimacy. The other rebukes him. This other guy is not getting what he deserves; he is guilty of the crime of driving while black, of political machinations. Jesus, I want to be innocent. Remember that. Remember me. It has been said that God does not need us to be willing to follow, but hopes we will be willing to be made willing; God hopes we will be open enough to God's graceful, joyful, and gentle coaxing so that we can follow.

Jesus, remember me. Remember why I made the choices I made that were so sour. Have compassion. Jesus's reply? Today you will join me in paradise, which really means "in the loveliest garden." In early Christian tradition, Jesus dies atop Adam's remains, Adam's skull. The Skull. There Jesus plants a new garden—a paradise—and invites his fellow crucified to join him in both the planting and the harvest. And he invites us.

57

Idle Tales

Luke 24:1–35

It is difficult to be amazed by a story that seems knitted into our cultural DNA. The element of surprise is critical as we approach a familiar story, not only to understanding the characters, but also to understanding Luke's Gospel. The women who have economically supported Jesus and followed him for as long as the men, the women who dared to sit at his feet and stand at the foot of the cross, are the first to know. They are the first witnesses to the resurrection because they put themselves at the tomb, to show their care for the Jesus they had come to know and love as well as to grieve the end of their relationship with him. Anointing the dead was not necessarily women's work, which would otherwise explain why the men stay behind; the women have the courage to go out and visit, even at personal risk, the man they knew and loved. They find the tomb already opened and the body missing. They do not quite understand. They had made themselves vulnerable just by going and then he wasn't there. The folk in dazzling clothes say that the Jesus they have followed asks them to follow again, to leave Jerusalem and go to Galilee. The women are the first evangelists. They tell the other disciples that Jesus and their relationship with him has a future and not just a past. Their revelation is received as an old wives' tale.

An unfounded fable. Women's talk. An emotional story. The disciples flatten the news and hope of a resurrection with a stereotype. Peter investigates. One wonders what would have happened had he not taken the risk to trust someone culturally untrustworthy with news bigger than he could hope for. Luke continues to offer us an invitation. Throughout this Gospel, Luke and Jesus *and* God resist stereotypes. Women, who were not allowed to study the Torah but were allowed by the living Jesus to sit at his feet, are the first witnesses to a new and future relationship with Jesus and God. We often hold on to idle tales instead of looking for the presence of the risen Lord, to being open to following Jesus for the sake of ourselves and the world.

Curiously, idle tales become idol tales. The disciples almost miss out and we do too. Do we discount stories of resurrection, of new life, of reconciliation as idle tales, and often miss theologies of liberation and care along the way? The church of my youth told the following idle tales without objection: Women are equal to men, except not really because they can't be ministers/priests and men are the spiritual heads of households. God loves us, but doesn't really like us. We all have to believe the same principles to be a real church. Some questions are too irreverent to be asked. Churches are places where we all agree to agree. Idle tales. Idol tales. Isn't God calling us out of idolatry by asking us to follow the risen Jesus to somewhere other than where we are today?

The walk to Emmaus. The two friends pass on the disturbing events, this idle tale and their objection to it, to the stranger. Did they even bother to look at the stranger? How did they fail to recognize Jesus? Similarly, do we miss him in one another, in strangers or "servants," because we never even look? We see what we believe. We are tied to our phones or to the pictures in our heads. Jesus the stranger opens the truth, hope, and miracle of resurrection. They do not get it until he does something very simple. He shares bread with them. Is this the first time they look at his face, the first time they are not preoccupied with their own grief, their own idle and idol tales, to hear God's story in another? Do we offer God's counternarratives to idle tales of our own and our world every time we share nourishment with another, to notice them, to make eye contact? Does stopping to help change a flat tire bring new life for the world? Sharing ourselves edits the cultural narrative of scarcity and competition and might just give us a glimpse, if we dare to follow, of the kin-dom that God has in store for us.

58

A New Call

Luke 24:36–52

Throughout the Holy Scripture and throughout history, several people have been resuscitated, but only Jesus has been resurrected. The difference? Resuscitation is when life leaves a person and an intervention happens and life is restored. Defibrillators do this. Lazarus is resuscitated in the Gospel of John after being dead four days. The resuscitated gain their life back, but only temporarily; they will die again.

Jesus is unique. He will never die again and, unlike the resuscitated, his wounds will not go away. The resurrection claim of the earliest disciples was countered by Jewish, Greek, and Roman critics. *A stolen body.* The disciples stole Jesus's body from the tomb, claimed he had come back, and invented the ascension so that no one could prove it thereafter. *Mistaken identity.* Jesus was not crucified, but rather someone who looked like Jesus. Let's call this one "Brian." After laying low for a few days while Brian took the penalty, Jesus came out of hiding and pronounced his resurrection. *The ghostly vision.* The disciples only thought they were seeing Jesus when, in fact, they were only hallucinating, projecting, or seeing a spirit that had no corporeal reality. *The swoon theory.* Jesus did not die on the cross, but rather swooned into a low-grade coma and then woke up three days later.

Luke takes on all of these arguments at the same time. Jesus eats, as ghosts do not. Jesus has wounds, disproving the mistaken identity theory.

He talks and can be touched, resisting the stolen body theory. The resurrection of the body is one of the most critical elements of our faith, embedded in the Apostles' and Nicene Creeds.

Luke is not interested in the historicity of the resurrected body to check a box, but because the God of second chances does not wait for heaven, and neither should we. Neither can we if we are to resist the idle and idol tales of yesterday. We are called, as the disciples were, to be witnesses, "martyrs" in Greek, of the physical resurrection of Jesus—of the infinite God's presence in the finite—of immanence.

Jesus opens the minds of the disciples to read scripture not as a litmus test, but as revealing God's presence and salvation in time itself, in the world, in us. We can read scripture in ways that resist resurrection or we can follow the resurrected Jesus as we read, mark, and inwardly digest God's Word. Holy Scripture points to God's fundamental love, curiosity, and care for humanity, a care so deep that the incarnation occurred. *We* are to be witnesses that death is not final. We are to be witnesses that God will take care of us after we die, and also now while we live. We are to be witnesses that vulnerability in love is God's way.

Jesus is lifted up; his wounded body ascends to heaven. God reveals that vulnerability has always been a part of who God is. The Ascension completes what the Incarnation initiated: the human experience is mysteriously near and dear to God's own heart and eternal identity. The disciples are to be witnesses of the real and full presence of the resurrected God in each aspect of living.

We are called to live into resurrection and reconciliation with one another, to read the scriptures in ways that affirm life and counter oppression, degradation, and judgment.

In a few days' time (Acts 2), the Holy Spirit will blow into town and fill the disciples with a second wind. Pentecost is not merely a historical event; it is a way of life. Breathe in God's life and breathe it out on one another, across linguistic and cultural and denominational barriers. The season after Pentecost is only ordinary time if we settle for that. Being called a disciple of Christ is anything but ordinary.